LANKAN
FILLING
STATION

LANKAN FILLING
O TAMA CAREY

'The thing that makes you most Sri Lankan is not your father's surname or the holy place where you kneel, nor the smile you plaster on your face to hide your fears. It is the knowing of other Lankans and the knowing of those Lankans' Lankans.'

Shehan Karunatilaka,
The Seven Moons of Maali Almeida

'It reflects the double standard chefs of colour face when cooking from their own heritage – they're expected to miraculously nail someone else's ideal of their cuisine, instead of being allowed honest, evolving ideas about the food.'

Lee Tran Lam

Hardie Grant
BOOKS

STAR BRAND

SPRINKLER
BOOSTER
FIRE
HYDRANT

INTRODUCTION

Hello and welcome. I would never be so bold as to assume I know why you are here in my book, but I can let you know what to expect. This is not a traditional Sri Lankan cookbook (although some dishes in here are), it's a collection of recipes that at their heart, whether by flavour or idea, are connected to Sri Lanka but are still distinctly Australian.

There is great beauty in cooking traditionally and playing by the rules, studying the flavours and techniques of a country and exploring their origins. It's like when you meet someone new who you want to be friends with. First you become shyly enamoured, but then you start learning about where they came from and suddenly you gain a deeper understanding of them and everything makes more sense. This gathering of knowledge can be a never-ending process and the more involved you get, the more you will realise how much you don't understand and how much more there is to know. Food, like people, can simultaneously be both very complicated and simple. However, as you delve deeper and master the ways, it becomes easier to swerve and adapt without losing integrity. Learn the rules first, and then you can play.

The circumstances that got me here are many and varied. I have a Sri Lankan mother, was born in Australia and am lucky to have grown up with a hungry family, talented in both cooking and eating. Flavour was always important and, even as a child disinterested in eating, I was exposed to foods from many cultures. Very early in my life, I accidentally started a career in cooking. I began in London, where the work started as just a means to an end. I was on my first solo travel adventure, needed money and serendipitously found work in a kitchen. I thought I'd been hired as a dishwasher but nope, it was straight into the fire, so to speak, and there I have stayed.

Back in Australia I continued my learning, first at an excellent French bistro, serving the classics, and then to a super cool little Japanese place where I was again thrown in the deep end. After that I chased the smoke of the wok at Billy Kwong, one of the first places I properly experienced the idea of fusing Asia with modern Australia. After that, there were a few lovely years of roaming and doing bits and pieces, some of which was occasionally cooking at a small Italian wine bar with a tiny kitchen and unforgettable food. The owner became my mate and, when he wanted to open a new place, Berta, he said I could have free reign of the kitchen. The only rule was that it had to be Italian. I agreed, but as I discovered my own cooking style, I found it impossible to shake all the flavours that had got me there: my French training, my love of all things Asian and my Sri Lankan roots.

Finally, my obsession with curry leaves could no longer be contained and I opened my very own Sri Lankan restaurant, called Lankan Filling Station (LFS). At first, I felt woefully underqualified to be presenting this food. I struggled with the notion of authenticity, despite my heritage and all the time I have spent on the island, researching, eating and learning. I have squatted on dirt floors in semi-darkness with a scary looking, slightly blunt knife held upright between my toes, learning how to chop chillies by pressing them down onto the blade (a confusing upside method). I have sat on a wooden bench with a coconut grater attached and feebly attempted to grate a coconut. I have cooked things in fires, and I have made mistakes. All these times I have been overseen by excellent women who have laughed at me, held my hand, fed me and taught me, often despite having no common language. Authentic and traditional experiences to be sure, but by no means the only answer when it comes to food. Besides, if I tried to cook barefoot in a kitchen here, there would be trouble.

For a while there, I did a lot of grappling with the big, serious ideas of authenticity, tradition and cultural appropriation and how the restaurant was perceived. I even wrote a cookbook, *Lanka Food* (LF), to learn more about where the recipes we were cooking really came from. It was an interesting time. Some Lankans said the food we cooked reminded them of home; others said the food had been dumbed down to suit the Western palate. One person even accused me of cultural appropriation. It was very confusing.

But then this is what comes next, the evolution of my version of Sri Lankan food. It celebrates the cuisine and weaves in elements from different parts of the world equally, embracing the glorious way of food that is so distinctly and irreverently done in Australia. It shows foundational recipes and flavours and explains how to bend them to create something else entirely. And hopefully this will be a guide, showing you how to get there yourself, how, with the help of some curry leaves and coconut, you too can become a little bit Sri Lankan. So please interpret these recipes how you will, go wild, have fun, experiment. All you need to do is please your own tastebuds, and damn to the rules.

A note on recipes

It may seem a little ridiculous to bring this up now, but really, the whole concept of a recipe is somewhat flawed. As a cook, whatever type of restaurant you work in, there will be recipes. Whether they're printed and laminated in a folder, written on a scrap of paper or whispered to you over a hot stove, there are always instructions. And the beauty of the professional kitchen is that there will always be someone there, showing you how, having a taste and hopefully approving of what you do. It's a tangible experience rather than just words on paper.

Many years ago, I started writing a food column. I have a very distinct memory of sitting down to write my first recipe. I can't remember exactly what it was for, but I do remember the ingredients calling for one long red chilli. And this one little thing stopped me in my tracks. What if someone only had small red chillies to use? Maybe this wouldn't be enough or maybe, because they were smaller, it would be too hot and too much. What if my idea of mildly hot was someone else's idea of burning heat?

This confusion can be applied to each and every ingredient in a recipe. What size is a medium onion anyway? What if your spices are a bit stale and one teaspoon of fennel seeds doesn't give enough flavour? What if tomatoes are out of season and they taste flat or too watery? What if the brand of coconut milk you use is a bit too sweet or not rich enough? What if your burner on a low heat is far hotter than mine? How does weather affect your ingredients, or cook time, or the flavour of your produce? Ovens are even more of a mystery – I would suggest very few cook in the same way. And most importantly, any hand that touches food is going to impart its own flavour or style or feel.

Can you see the futility?

And so, because I am not here with you, standing beside and showing you, we have to rely on other things. My ability to write clear and detailed recipes that make sense (if I fail in this, please take it up with my publisher ...). There is the concept of assumed knowledge and common sense, which one always hopes for. There is the use of scales to give very specific amounts (I know some people in home kitchens find this a bit annoying, but it really is the most accurate way).

But, my main desire is that you use your own senses, taste and adjust, smell and modify, touch and adapt. Because there is no such thing as foolproof, and there will always be endless interpretations.

And then, the idea of writing a cookbook doesn't seem quite so futile.

INGREDIENTS & SPICES

When playing with food from a different culture, the first step is the ingredients. There's always something specific to each place, a type of produce you don't find elsewhere, some particular way of using it or a dominant ingredient that gets used abundantly. But ingredients alone don't make it so – you can't just add a curry leaf and call it Sri Lankan. There are methods of cooking and there's also the place you are in. Which begs the question, can you truly cook traditional food outside of its birthplace? (Please debate among yourselves.) And the flip side to that: is any Sri Lankan food I cook here also, by definition, slightly Australian?

Ingredients in particular are tricky, and I'm not talking about the hard-to-find, only-in-Sri-Lanka ones. I'm talking about the basics. Let's look at onions. What cuisine doesn't use these? Take normal red ones, for example. The ones you find in Sri Lanka have a vastly different flavour to the Australian ones, despite them looking the same. Lankan red onions are far sweeter and have none of the sharp sulphuric aftertaste that ours do. I have eaten dishes on the island filled with large, barely cooked wedges of onion that have been delicious, but if I tried that here it would all be too much. So you see, even the basics are going to give you trouble if you have the mindset of strict replication.

This alone can be the starting point for fusion in food. You use the best quality ingredients available wherever you happen to be and adapt them into a recipe in an appropriate manner. The other key is looking at flavour profiles. A good example is Maldive fish, a dried smoked fish from the Maldives, which is integral to Sri Lankan food. It's used to give extra protein in the vegetable-heavy food of the country, but also as a seasoning to add flavour, depth and umami much in the same way as fish sauce is used in Thailand, katsuobushi is used in Japan or colaturra is used in Italy. And see, does this not make your head explode with all the possibilities this could lead to?

There are a few specifically Sri Lankan and Australian items within this book that, although there are substitutes, are better when you have the real deal. I've summarised these overleaf. Luckily, most of these shouldn't be too hard to track down, especially with the help of the internet. And again, it's a matter of taste. There are probably one billion types of canned coconut milk and cream. Maybe you have a favourite, or maybe you will use what I suggest? Or maybe you will be one of those excellent humans who wants to grate and then make their own. Whichever you choose, the result is going to be different (please refer back to the futility of recipes, page 11).

5b
11
5a
15
5c
22
5e
37
13
5f
5d
30
a
30
b
4b
7
10
4a
EXTRA SPECIAL
ARRACK
8b
1
38
24
6
LION
2
14
17

9b
9c
9a
12
3
9d
31
DELICIOUS
ROSE BRAND
35a
21
34
16
27
25
23
36
20
28d
40
19
28b
33
26
28a
28c
29
18
39
8f
32

1 ARRACK

Arrack is the main spirit of Sri Lanka, very unlike the more commonly known Middle Eastern drink of the same name, which has a strong aniseed flavour. It is made by 'tapping' the fruit of a coconut palm to gather the sap. As this sap ferments, it becomes slightly boozy and is then known as toddy. This ferment is then distilled to make the hard liquor known as arrack. Colonists dismissed arrack as a crude drink fit only for the natives and not nearly as good as whisky, despite being made in a similar way. It's had a hard time shaking this reputation – sometimes understandably so, as some versions as are all kick and no flavour. Like anything, though, find a well-made version and you will enjoy a smooth, sippable booze with hints of sweetness and subtle undertones of coconut.

2 BETEL LEAVES

In Australia, betel is an ingredient used mostly in Thai cooking; it is a dark leaf with an almost waxy texture and a nice amount of bitterness. In Sri Lanka though, the bitterness of what they call a betel leaf is out of control. It's not something to be eaten; rather, it's wrapped around a betel nut and chewed as a stimulant then spat out, leaving a red stain where it lands. I tried it once with a very cute nana half my size who was highly amused by the horror on my face as I chewed. If you are in Sri Lanka, ask for a pepper leaf, which is the same as what we call a betel leaf.

3 BUFFALO CURD

This is one of those tricky ingredients whose specific flavour and method of creation is particular to the island. It's made with buffalo milk and natural cultures and set into unglazed clay pots, creating a yoghurt that is thick, tangy and very delicious. Nothing in Australia tastes quite the same, but we have found a product called buffalo curd, which is firmly set, more like a cheese. It's not the same, but it's what I'm referring to here when I say buffalo curd. If you are looking at Lankan recipes elsewhere and see a reference to buffalo curd, substitute with a thick Greek yoghurt.

4 CARDAMOM

Green cardamom (a) is native to Sri Lanka, where it is used more often than its relative, brown cardamom (b), which you find a lot in Indian cooking and has a far more intense flavour (it's hectic). I only use green and I like to have both the pods and seeds at hand. The seeds give a stronger, more pure flavour, especially when pounded, but the pods are good when you want to infuse a more subtle flavour and they can easily be fished out or avoided when eating. Crunching on a whole pod can be an alarming experience. It has a menthol-like quality and adds depth to a dish, yet its alluring sweetness is what I love. Five pods are about equal to a gram of seeds.

5 CHILLIES – FRESH AND DRIED

Chilli in all its glorious forms is so integral to the food of Sri Lanka, it's shocking to realise it is a relative newcomer to the island, introduced by the Portuguese around the fifteenth-ish century. These days, you'll find some form of chilli in almost every Sri Lankan dish, either dried (a) as a spice (b) or fresh, in both cooked and raw dishes. A chilli's flavour can be almost as distinctive as its heat. Generally, the long ones are less hot than the small, fiery ones. When dried, it moves into the category of a spice and can be used as a powder, a flake or as whole dried chillies. And of course, any version or batch of these will be slightly different, with varying degrees of heat.

Each form of chilli will give you a different version of heat. Fresh will depend on the variety and whether or not it is cooked, and dried can also go in many directions. In these recipes I specify either long chillies – red (c) or green (d) – usually for a milder heat, or bird's eye – also red (e) or green (f) – for a more intense heat. When using fresh chilli, I never remove the seeds unless specifically stated. With dried, the general rule is that chilli powder gives a heavy, rounded flavour while chilli flakes or pieces give a sharper, more lively heat. But again, go with your taste. You can find chilli powders that are sweeter rather than hotter, or you can wuss out even more and just use less, or none at all.

6 CINNAMON

The biggest challenge in my quest to be Sri Lankan has been learning to love cinnamon. It is prevalent in the food and native to the island, where it's considered the best quality in the world. In savoury dishes, cinnamon adds depth and a gentle sweetness, but it's equally happy in sweet things too. And it is beautiful to look at, especially when you see it as it's first traded: long sticks, around 1.2 m (3.9 ft) as a standard, bundled together and all formed by hand. Although at first glance it looks like a tight concentric circle, cinnamon is actually the outer layer of bark. Large pieces are used to envelop smaller pieces, which are then rolled and packed and rolled some more until tightly formed. The smell of fresh cinnamon is a delight, as is the scent of the leaves, which are also great for adding flavour, particularly when they are fresh. And if you happen to be cooking dinner on a cinnamon plantation, as I have, this comes in very handy.

7 CLOVES

Cloves are not native to Sri Lanka, but have been cultivated there for so long they are now deeply embedded in the food. They have a strong flavour with a beautiful scent, medicinal yet sweet. And they pair very nicely with cardamom and cinnamon, making for a very fine trio. Cloves are very bold though, and can easily overpower a dish unless used judiciously.

8 COCONUT

If you removed all forms of coconut from the island, Sri Lanka would probably cease to exist. As well as being a staple in the cuisine, the rest of the tree is used for everything from building homes and roofs to making utensils (f), bowls and brooms. Whether in a city or a village, it would be impossible to walk more than a few steps in any direction without seeing the palm in any one of its many forms. Its importance cannot be understated.

– COCONUT WATER

Coconut water (a) is excellent to drink. Roadside stalls generally sell two types: a young coconut, which is green in colour, sweet and probably the flavour most commonly found all over the world; a young king coconut, on the other hand, is distinctly orange in colour (hence the name, thambali, which is Sinhalese for orange) and my favourite. They have a slightly savoury flavour that is hard to explain unless you drink one. Equally refreshing is the water that comes from a mature coconut, the ones used for grating.

– GRATED COCONUT

Fresh grated coconut (b) comes from the flesh of a mature coconut. It is used to make sambols and sweets, and added to curries as a thickener. Scraping coconuts for your own home cooking is not as tricky as it sounds, though it is labour intensive. You just need the right tools, a bit of patience and access to mature coconuts. But no one will think less of you if you buy freshly grated frozen coconut, which can be found at Sri Lankan or Thai grocers. The quality will vary, but it is a perfectly adequate substitute. If neither of these is an option, you will have to make do with desiccated coconut. Add 40 ml (1¼ fl oz) of warm water or milk for each 100 g (3½ oz) desiccated coconut, mix thoroughly with your hands and let it sit for at least 5 minutes before using. It is the least best option, but it will do.

– COCONUT MILK (AND CREAM)

Coconut milk (c) is made by adding warm or hot water to grated coconut, mixing it and squeezing it before straining. The resulting liquid is the milk. In Sri Lanka, this step is repeated up to three times, each batch used for different preparations, as the milk becomes more diluted with each pressing. They don't talk so much of actual coconut cream (the solid fat that rises to the top when the milk is left to sit); rather, they refer to the first, second or third press. That said, I assume most people will buy coconut milk rather than making their own. Supermarkets carry a large range of both coconut milk and cream, which can vary enormously in thickness and flavour. The brand you choose will make a difference to the final product. My advice is to go with your taste preference: if you want a richer curry, add more milk or cream; if you want a thinner version, add more water. In my recipes I use a particular brand of coconut cream, Kara, and dilute it to my needs.

– COCONUT OIL

Coconut oil (d) is one of the most commonly used fats in Sri Lankan cooking and, depending on the zeitgeist, is either extremely healthful or very bad for you. I have been told that when it's used to cook rice there's some clever scientific thing that happens that reduces the calories in the rice and makes it better for you. This is an interesting fact that possibly explains why you can still be healthy in Sri Lanka, where the average rice portions in a meal are ginormous. It's one of those clever symbiotic relationships in food. At its worst, it can be overpowering, overused and, in the heat of the island, can turn rancid. However, like cinnamon, I have come around to it. There are now many cold-pressed versions available, which still have the distinct smell but with a more delicate flavour. So I say use away, and keep your vegan friends happy.

– COCONUT VINEGAR

Coconut vinegar (e) is the sap of the flower of the coconut palm, left to naturally ferment for up to a year. It is usually a little cloudy in appearance, and the flavour can vary depending on the brand. The one we use is very vinegary with a strong fermented taste and needs to be used judiciously.

9 CORIANDER SEEDS AND LEAVES

Coriander seeds (a) form the base of most curry powders and are therefore an important part of the cuisine. They have a mild, earthy flavour with hints of citrus, and provide a beautiful base for other, more pungent spices. Weirdly, despite the prevalence of the seeds, the leaves are used far less than I would expect. The leaves are delicious, and provide a fresh feel and a calming note to spiced foods. When I use fresh coriander (cilantro) in a recipe I try to incorporate the whole bunch. Leaves (b) are picked – not individually but with a bit of stem (c) – and the remaining stem and root (d) are used in pastes and cooking.

10 CUMIN SEEDS

Cumin is native to the Middle East, but is now also grown in Sri Lanka. It is mostly ground into curry powders to help blend and balance flavours, and rarely used whole. Cumin has a strong, slightly bitter flavour and is best used in moderation, but what I love is that it is so savoury.

11 CURRY LEAVES

Fresh curry leaves are probably the only ingredient I would say you can't substitute, and can't do without.

I would be lost without these glorious leaves. The trees are from the citrus family, which is why they are so zingy and their scent so hunger-inducing. Luckily for us, they are becoming easier to find, even appearing in supermarkets. They are also very easy to grow. They do not dry very well, however, so if you have a glut, I'd freeze them or make a batch of butter. Some recipes say you can substitute with bay leaves, which I think is a bit of nonsense, but I do love the flavour of these two leaves together – not interchangeable but with similar notes.

12 FENNEL SEEDS

Like coriander, the seeds of fennel are used in Sri Lankan cooking far more than the fresh bulb, which I am not sure I have ever actually seen on the island. (That always makes me wonder: how do they get the seeds?) That said, even the seeds aren't used a lot, but I really love their sweet aniseed flavour, which is amplified and gains a hint of nuttiness when toasted.

13 FENUGREEK SEEDS

Fenugreek are usually soaked in water before being added to dishes. They mainly act as a thickener, but also have bitter digestive qualities. My Nan told me to use them in any dish that contains pork for this very reason.

14 GHEE

Ghee is not actually that prevalent in Sri Lankan cooking, but I use it a lot as I love its flavour. Ghee is basically a form of clarified butter, a process whereby the fat in butter is separated from the milk solids. In ghee, this process is taken a bit further, until the milk solids are slightly cooked. This gives ghee a beautiful, caramelised flavour, buttery and sweet, which is even better. When we make it at the restaurant, we take it even further, to the edge of burnt to bring out these flavours even more. If you don't have ghee, you can cheat a little and use half butter and half neutral oil to get a similar effect.

15 GINGER

This little rhizome is an important part of Lankan cuisine. It's used both fresh and dried, as a spice. We went through so much fresh ginger at LFS that we often saved the skin and dried it to make our own ginger powder.

16 GOTU KOLA/PENNYWORT

This little beauty of a leaf, also known as penny worth, is native to both Asia and Australia. It's little and bitter and delicious, very good for you, and quite easy to grow.

17 JACKFRUIT

Jackfruit deserves a mention, even though it only appears in this book once. They are a beauty of a thing and can grow extremely large. In Sri Lanka this fruit is used from when it's young and unripe all the way through to fully ripe, with each stage having a different name – polos when very young, kos when used in cooking, say for a curry, and varaka when they are fully ripe and sweet. The fruit is highly perfumed with hints of pineapple, banana and a slightly fermented note. And the seeds get used too. It's a clever thing.

18 JAGGERY (AND KITHUL)

Jaggery refers to any unrefined palm, corn or date sap that is treated and used as a sweetener. Most Asian countries have their own version of this, with varying levels of sweetness, ranging in colour from quite pale to golden. Sri Lankan jaggery is generally quite dark, with a flavour that is sweet but not sugary – more like molasses, with a hint of savoury smokiness. It is made from the sap of a coconut palm, either a palmyrah or kithul palm (the latter is believed to produce the more superior product). The sap is collected from the flower of the tree and boiled down to a dark, sticky consistency. At this stage, while it is still pourable, it's known as kithul, kithul pani (pani is also the name for honey) or kithul treacle. Sadly, many of the commercial varieties use sugar syrup, both to make it cheaper but also to stabilise it – as a natural product it is very volatile and prone to over-fermenting. But if you are ever lucky enough to try a fresh, unadulterated version you are in for a real treat. I got to taste some recently at the home of a maker. We sat outside on plastic chairs, a cup of black tea in one hand, the other holding a saucer of this beautiful amber liquid and took alternate sips. It was fragrant, delicate and aromatic, and unlike anything I'd ever tasted.

After it has reduced further it is poured into halved coconut shells and left to set; at this point it is known as jaggery (palm sugar). It becomes quite hard, and sometimes a little crumbly. When using it in recipes it's best to use a cleaver or heavy knife to chop it into smaller pieces or coarsely grate it. Grating is a little more time consuming but, especially for sweet preparations, it will melt and blend more easily. It is an unrefined product and therefore better for you than refined sugars, but it is still a sugar. It can be used anywhere you want some sweetness.

19 KANGAROO

Kangaroos are native to Australia and have been a source of protein for far longer than any introduced animal. And really, if we live here, it does make sense to eat them. I do have to admit though, they are not my favourite eating animal. The meat is a little gamey and super lean, which means that unless it's cooked properly it can become quite tough and chewy. However, as always, if you deal with it properly it can be a real treat.

20 KARKALLA

This little succulent is native to Australia and is also known as pigface or beach banana. That last name is particularly apt, as its green sprigs are a bit banana shaped, and the plant grows in coastal areas. It has a fleshy texture, with a delightful crunchy juiciness and a subtle salty flavour. It can be used both raw and cooked.

21 LEMONGRASS

This plant is native to India and widely used throughout Asia. The long stalk has a slightly bulbous base, and that's where all the flavour is – citrusy, zesty and quite sharp. Lemongrass is very fibrous, so it's best used either chopped finely, pounded or by bruising the stalk and throwing it in whole to infuse the flavour, then removing it before serving. The top stalky bit can be used in stocks and to make syrups.

22 LIMES

Citrus fruits are common to most of the world, their history a tangle of interbreeding. Limes are an excellent example of such hybrids, and are an important ingredient in Lankan cooking, lending their sourness to curries and sambols. The limes found in Sri Lanka have the same flavour as limes everywhere (I assume, not having tasted limes everywhere in the world), but they are usually smaller in size, sometimes with a more orange hue to their green skin.

23 MALDIVE FISH

Along with curry leaves, this is the ingredient that I think makes Sri Lankan food distinctly Sri Lankan. It's also an ingredient that can be stretched and used in many untraditional ways. As the name suggests, this is a fish product that comes from the nearby Maldive islands, usually bonito or slipjack tuna, that is dried and smoked until it becomes very hard, almost like wood. It is usually sold in chips or flakes, and can be found in Sri Lankan and some Indian grocers. The flavour is strong, but not nearly as stinky as many other Asian dried shrimp pastes or fish sauces. It can be pounded until fine and mixed into sambols, or the flakes can be added to curries and vegetable dishes. It works as a thickener, an added source of protein and as a way to balance flavour, much as you would with fish sauce. Use it subtly to add a salty and smoky umami note, or more liberally as a flavour in its own right.

24 MORU CHILLIES

These little beauties are truly a gift of Sri Lankan cuisine. They're made by taking whole chillies, usually green, soaking them in whey or yoghurt to ferment, sun drying them, then deep-frying and serving them as an accompaniment to a rice and curry meal. They are salty, sour and crisp, and offer extra excitement as their heat can be like a lucky dip, ranging from mild to hiccup-inducing. We've served some batches that were so hot I looked out into a restaurant full of customers, all with tears in their eyes. Traditionally served as is, at LFS we slipped them in anywhere we could, and found many exciting uses for them. They were also very good as a seasoning for pizza.

25 MUSTARD SEEDS

When raw, the seeds are flavourless and odourless, becoming pungent and spicy when cooked or pounded. The flavour varies greatly depending on how they are used. In Sri Lankan cuisine you'll find them in mustards, pickles, mustard oil (for eating and medicinal purposes) and in curry bases. The practice of tempering is often applied to these seeds, but care must be taken, as the flavour becomes very bitter and unpleasant if the seeds are overcooked. I tend to favour black mustard seeds, but using brown seeds instead won't make a huge difference.

26 NIGELLA SEEDS

Native to western Asia and southern Europe, these little black seeds (often referred to as black cumin) are grown and used extensively in India. They are less common in Sri Lankan cooking, but they do appear in some of the curry powders. They are sharp, peppery, slightly nutty and strong, with an excellent savoury flavour and good digestive qualities.

27 NUTMEG

Nutmeg is the dried fruit of a tree. The outside covering, known as mace, is often used in Lankan cooking; the inside is the very hard oval shape we know as nutmeg. In Lankan cuisine, nutmeg is mainly used in desserts, but some also appears in one of the curry powders (page 29).

28 ONIONS

The names, varieties and flavour of onions vary depending on where you are. In Australia we are mostly confined to red (a), brown (b) and white, which is quite basic, or French or banana eschalots or shallots (c) (same thing, two names). My favourite little ones, which get used a lot in Sri Lanka as well, are the tiny red ones. In Australia they're called Thai eschalots. They are sweet and excellent, although incredibly time-consuming to peel. There are also spring onions, also called shallots (d) – the long thin ones – and there are red and green varieties of these, too. And then the other fresh spring onions, which look the same but are more bulbous at the end. The most confusing thing about this is the names, which vary from place to place, and even state to state.

29 PAPRIKA

Paprika is a spice made in the same way as chilli powder, but from sweet rather than hot capsicums (bell peppers) or chillies. Originally North American, it was adopted by the Portuguese, which is how it found its way to Sri Lanka. There are hot and smoked varieties, but sweet paprika is what's used in Lankan cuisine, bringing colour and flavour without the excessive heat. It's a good way to start people on their chilli appreciation journey, much like using training wheels. If you use both chilli and sweet paprika, you can adjust the ratios to suit your heat preference without messing with the overall flavour too much.

30 PEPPER – WHITE AND BLACK AND LONG

Native to the coast of India but widely grown in Sri Lanka, pepper, prior to the introduction of chilli, was the main source of heat in food. As such, it gets used far more liberally in Sri Lankan cuisine than as the gentle seasoning it's relegated to in Western cuisine, and is treated more like other spices, as a distinct flavour unto itself.

Pepper is a great enabler and when used in combination with other spices, it allows the body to more readily absorb their medicinal properties. The heat from black pepper (a) is deep, earthy and pungent. White pepper (b) (which is simply black pepper treated differently) offers a zippier version of the warmth of black pepper. Although white pepper is less common in Sri Lanka, you will find it throughout this book because I love its flavour. And then there's long black pepper (vine pepper), which is actually a different plant but from the same family. It has a strong perfumed floral flavour with a numbing quality similar to Sichuan pepper (which is from a different plant and a different family).

31 PEPPERBERRY

And, as we talk of peppers, there's this one too, again a different plant and family from the vine peppers. Pepperberry is also known as Tasmanian or mountain pepper, and is native to Australia. Both the leaves and berries are used, both dried, the berries treated in the same way as you would black pepper. However, they have an intense, mouth-numbing heat and a strong flavour, much like the above-mentioned Sichuan and long peppers. When ground, they become almost oily looking. We sometimes season our egg hoppers with them at the restaurant, even though it does leave a distinctive purple stain. This is a spice to be used in the same way you would any pepper, but more sparingly please, as it is quite hectic.

32 PIPIS

These shelled beauties are from the mollusc family, native to Australia, and also known as Coorong or Goolwa cockles. They are often used for bait, but personally, I would much rather eat them. They are similar to other shellfish like vongole and clams – and even mussels at a stretch – in the way that they are used. They can be quite sandy and need to be purged; they don't live for very long once caught and usually they will pop their shells open when cooked. Pipis are one of those things you have to work for – a little bit of delicate flesh hidden inside a shell. They are very good matched with strong flavours, and best eaten delicately with your fingers.

33 RAMPE

Native to southeast Asia and more commonly known as pandan, these long aromatic leaves are a dark to light green, and the flavour is sweet with hints of vanilla. In Sri Lanka, dried pandan is usually added to curry powders, and the fresh leaves are cut into pieces and cooked with rice or in curries. It is there to infuse flavour, not to eat. For some reason pandan essence, which is used in other Asian cuisines for desserts, doesn't really get a look-in, which I think is a missed opportunity as it makes for an excellent addition to sweet dishes. When using fresh rampe, my tip is to tie it into a knot before you add it – that way it's contained, and easy to fish out.

34 RICE

When it comes to important ingredients in Sri Lanka, rice is right up there with coconut. So many meals are rice with something, rather than rice being a side dish and, as a Westerner, it's almost alarming to see how much rice is served as a portion. Sambols and relishes are referred to as 'rice pullers', the idea being that they provide flavour to help you eat more rice. The political history and the very landscape of the island are intertwined with rice cultivation. This is a very big subject – there's too much to go into here, and it's all quite serious, so let's simply talk briefly of the types used.

Basmati rice appears quite a lot in Sri Lanka, but the two native types are samba, a short-grain white rice, and red rice, a dark rice, also short-grain. There are many different varietals of both types, and they both have the benefit of being more healthful and nutritious than basmati and also, in many areas, much more suited to cultivation on the island. A good substitute for samba, is koshihikari, a Japanese varietal and also one of my favourites. Sushi rice is another that will work well in these recipes.

35 ROSE – WATER, ESSENCE AND SYRUP

Too much rose in any of its forms is a sickly, overpowering experience, but used correctly, rose is a fragrant delight, and one used a lot in Sri Lanka. The only difference between a water and an essence is clear from their names: the water offers a more subtle flavouring than the thick, rich flavour you get from an essence. However, both should be used with caution. Rose syrup (a) is altogether different: a lurid pink concoction that is found all over Asia and most commonly used in Sri Lanka in its famous faluda, a weirdly refreshing milkshake drink.

36 SALTBUSH

There are a few plants that share this name but the one we most commonly eat in Australia is called Old Man Saltbush. It is a hardy native plant with slightly raggedy looking blue grey leaves and is eaten by both humans and animals. There is a slight fleshiness to the leaves texture and, as the name suggests, a saltiness to their flavour. There is also a little bit of bitter. They say you can eat the leaves raw, but I much prefer them cooked.

37 STAR ANISE

Star anise comes from a plant grown in India, which appears in dishes from the south of the country, although it is far less common in Sri Lanka. That said, my mum uses it in her Lankan cooking and it is one of my favourites, so here it is. Star anise has a sweet aniseed character with warmth, woodiness and pungency, and is excellent in both sweet and savoury preparations. To me, its flavour is almost a blend of fennel seeds, clove and cinnamon, which makes it highly appropriate for Sri Lankan flavours.

38 SPRATS

Sprats are the name given to a group of small fish from the herring family that are usually either dried or pickled, and are often confused with or used like a sardine or an anchovy. Just think, small oily fish … In Sri Lanka, it's often the dried one that is utilised, fried and prepared any number of ways, and that is what we mean in this book. Buying the dried version in an Asian grocer can be a bit of a lucky dip, as the flavour can range from subtle and delightfully salty to the stinky and strong end of the spectrum.

39 TAMARIND

Tamarind trees are not native to Sri Lanka, but are now grown all over the island. They have a beautiful canopy and are wonderful to sleep under. Part of the legume family, the fruit grows in long brown pods containing a soft, sweet, tangy pulp and large seeds. It can be eaten as a sweet and sour delicacy, sugared, or made into lollies, but it is more commonly partially dried (though still sticky) and used in savoury preparations. You can buy it in blocks, rehydrate it and sift out the many seeds, leaving a thick liquid, or buy it as a paste or concentrate. At LFS we used an extremely dark, very intense concentrate, but I don't believe it's readily available. For the purposes of this book, sometimes I use the block tamarind, but at other times I call for a concentrate or a paste. The paste is usually just a pre-done puree that can be easily found in an Asian grocer or supermarket. The intensity of flavour will vary quite a lot between a concentrate and any brand of paste, so be sure to be judicious. Remember, you can always add, but you can't take away …

40 TURMERIC

Native to southeast Asia, turmeric is a rhizome related to ginger. There are many similarities between these two friends, but also some distinct differences. Fresh turmeric is sharp, bitter, lively, a little earthy and very brightly coloured. In Sri Lanka it is more commonly used dried and ground, which intensifies the flavour, though it does lose its zing and can veer towards a dustier, earthier flavour. However, it doesn't lose its intense colour, which stains everything it touches. It is used extensively in Sri Lankan cooking, and many cookbooks claim it's there more for colour than flavour, but I disagree; the actual flavour can be underlying but it is very distinct and obvious, especially when overused. So too with the fragrance; it's there in the background, but can easily become all-pervading. Turmeric is well known for its health properties, especially when used with black pepper – a magic combination that can cure all.

8b
8e

8a
8c
8
8d
STAINLESS STEEL BLADES
ODIRIS
MADE IN CEYLON
SINCE 1952
SIYARATA DE SIRISAPA DE
ODIRIS
MODEL - B5
COCONUT GRATER
Manufactured by
ODIRIS ENGINEERING CO (PVT) LTD, DEHIWELA.
TEL: +94-112811063, FAX: +94-5341037, EMAIL: odiris@wow.lk

SPICES & CURRY POWDERS

Spices are ingredients too, but they are so important they get their own little section.

If you are playing around with Sri Lankan food you will quickly discover that spice mixes, curry powders or masalas (whatever you would like to call them; essentially, they're the same thing) are the base of all curries, and of many other dishes from the island. Speaking generally, there is much to be said about spices, with so much of human history traced in their wake. Explorers explored, fortunes were built, countries were conquered, and foods and flavours were exchanged all because of these beauties. With any particular mix, they have the power to define an entire country's cuisine.

And if you start delving into traditional foods, it soon becomes apparent that the combination of flavours often coincides with medicinal qualities, the two being so intertwined as to be impossible to separate. See how clever they are? And on top of all this, they also smell good. (At LFS, we toasted a few small pans of spices before every service and placed them in the bathroom for scent – nature's natural air freshener.)

But please don't be intimidated by their long history. Just think of them as any other ingredient, a flavour that you can add, then have a little taste. If you like it, add more; if you don't, don't. It is hard to tell the quality of a spice just by looking, but it is still important. The best way to get the good ones is to buy a good brand, or buy from somewhere that goes through spices quickly – even small, dried things can go stale. Spices are very volatile and once broken down, can very quickly lose their flavour, which is why I would never buy them pre-ground. Make your own spice blends from whole spices and I can guarantee you will be amazed at the difference. And if you have a well-stocked spice cupboard, it is fairly easy to grind them as you go, especially in a home kitchen where the quantities you will need should be manageable. There is also a big difference in the flavour of spices depending on how you treat them, whether ground or whole, toasted or not – toasting tends to bring out a stronger flavour. And there is usually a way that is more appropriate, which is the one that suits your taste.

To help you on your way, here are the recipes for the base curry powders.

They are divided by colour: white, brown, red and black. White powders are unroasted and don't contain any form of heat – no mustard, pepper or chilli. They are used for delicate dishes, subtle flavours and are very good as a gentle seasoning. Brown is the workhorse. The spices are toasted and well balanced; sometimes they are mild, sometimes less so. Brown is the most common powder (also called Ceylon, Sri Lankan or roasted curry powder) and can be used in most things. Red is usually hotter, but no less complex; the one here is laden with sweet spice. Black is very distinctive, a strong, robust powder, super-hot but with lots of sweet spices. Its strong flavour means this one is not to be used willy-nilly.

Please start with these as a way to learn but then, as you feel more comfortable, tweak to your taste and start sprinkling spices with gay abandon.

White curry powder

MAKES APPROXIMATELY 220 G (8 OZ)

This simple yet aromatic mix is bit like a curry powder in training. It is gentle and demure, with raw spices, but no less delicious for it. Use it to make white or yellow curries if you are going traditional, but also use it to season salads, cheese on toast, roasted vegetables or anything deep-fried. It is an excellent way to add some subtle spice without the heat, imparting a flavour that easily adapts without screaming Sri Lankan.

6 g (⅕ oz) picked curry leaves
70 g (2½ oz) coriander seeds
60 g (2 oz) fennel seeds
30 g (1 oz) nigella seeds
30 g (1 oz) cumin seeds
25 g (1 oz) turmeric powder

Place the curry leaves in a frying pan over a medium–high heat and cook gently for about 2 minutes. Reduce the heat a little and cook for another 1–2 minutes, until they are dry and toasted but not browned.

Allow the leaves to cool completely, then combine them with the remaining spices and grind to a fine powder. Store in an airtight container.

Brown curry powder

MAKES APPROXIMATELY 200 G (7 OZ)

This is our all-purpose friend, the mix that you can add to anything to make it really Sri Lankan. In traditional recipes this one also gets referred to as a toasted, Ceylon or Sri Lankan curry powder. It has plenty of flavour on its own, but you can also build other spices on top to send it in any direction you desire.

- 45 g (1½ oz) coriander seeds
- 30 g (1 oz) fennel seeds
- 30 g (1 oz) white peppercorns
- 30 g (1 oz) mustard seeds
- 20 g (¾ oz) cumin seeds
- 12 g (½ oz) picked curry leaves
- 1 g (1/32 oz) rampe (pandan) leaf, cut into 5 mm (¼ in) pieces
- 15 g (½ oz) cinnamon stick, roughly crushed
- 8 g (¼ oz) cardamom seeds
- 11 g (⅓ oz) turmeric powder
- 11 g (⅓ oz) chilli powder

Place a wide shallow frying pan over a medium–high heat, add the coriander and fennel seeds and toast gently, tossing regularly for even cooking. After about 2 minutes the spices will start popping and releasing their aromas. Reduce the heat and keep toasting for another 4–5 minutes, until the spices start to darken and the aroma becomes stronger and sweeter. Tip them into a bowl.

Add the peppercorns, mustard and cumin seeds, curry leaves and pandan to the pan and toast over a medium–high heat for 2 minutes, or until they start to pop. Reduce the heat and toast for another 2–3 minutes until the pepper smell is pronounced, the mustard seeds are not only popping but grey in colour, the cumin darkens, and the fresh leaves are dry. Tip them into the bowl with the coriander and fennel seeds.

Next, toast the cinnamon and cardamom seeds over a medium–low heat for 4–5 minutes, then add to the bowl with the other spices and allow to cool completely.

Grind to a fine powder and then mix through the turmeric and chilli powder. Store in an airtight container.

Red curry powder

MAKES APPROXIMATELY 150 G (5½ OZ)

This curry powder is a glorious, hot, red mix that is complex with sweet spices. Don't be scared by the long list of ingredients here. Apart from the curry leaves, it's just a matter of measuring and grinding – no tricky toasting of spices is required. If you are a bit scared of chilli, you can still use this. Just reduce the amount of chilli powder and up the paprika to maintain its excellent colour, sans heat.

5 g (⅕ oz) picked curry leaves
24 g (⅞ oz) sweet paprika
20 g (¾ oz) chilli powder
20 g (¾ oz) coriander seeds
15 g (½ oz) white peppercorns
13 g (½ oz) chilli flakes
12 g (½ oz) cumin seeds
10 g (½ oz) cardamom seeds
8 g (¼ oz) fennel seeds
8 g (¼ oz) cinnamon stick, roughly crushed
7 g (¼ oz) turmeric powder
5 g (⅕ oz) fenugreek seeds
3 g (⅒ oz) cloves
3 g (⅒ oz) star anise

Place the curry leaves in a frying pan over a medium–high heat and cook gently for about 2 minutes. Reduce the heat a little and cook for another 1–2 minutes until they are dry and toasted, but not browned.

Allow the leaves to cool completely, then combine them with the remaining spices and grind to a fine powder. Store in an airtight container.

Black curry powder

MAKES APPROXIMATELY 130 G (4½ OZ)

This is a complex powder, and probably the trickiest to make. It is also the most pungent. I once smoked out an entire warehouse while trying to make a small batch, and when it's being made in the restaurant I can smell it from several blocks away. One of my chefs would wrap a tea (dish) towel around her head, bandit style, to cook it. It has all the types of heat – pepper, mustard and chilli – and is laden with sweet spices. The trickiness comes with the toasting. You want to take the spices to the very edge of darkness before they tip over into bitter burntness. This gives complexity, and balances out all the sweet spices.

- 16 g (½ oz) coriander seeds
- 16 g (½ oz) cumin seeds
- 16 g (½ oz) nigella seeds
- 8 g (¼ oz) fennel seeds
- 16 g (½ oz) black peppercorns
- 20 g (¾ oz) mustard seeds
- 8 g (¼ oz) picked curry leaves
- 1 g (1⁄32 oz) rampe (pandan) leaf, cut into 5 mm (¼ in) pieces
- 5 g (⅕ oz) cardamom seeds
- 5 g (⅕ oz) cloves
- 3 g (1⁄10 oz) cinnamon stick, roughly crushed
- 16 g (½ oz) chilli powder
- 16 g (½ oz) chilli flakes
- 1 g (1⁄32 oz) freshly grated nutmeg

Place a wide shallow frying pan over a medium–high heat, add the coriander, cumin, nigella and fennel seeds and toast gently, tossing regularly for even cooking. After about 2 minutes the spices will start popping and releasing their aromas. Reduce the heat and keep toasting for another 6–7 minutes until the spices start to darken and the aroma becomes stronger and sweeter. Tip them into a bowl.

Add the peppercorns, mustard seeds, curry leaves, rampe (pandan) to the pan and toast over a medium–high heat for 2 minutes. Reduce the heat and toast for another 4–5 minutes, until the pepper smell is pronounced, the mustard seeds are popping and grey in colour and the fresh leaves are dark and dry. Tip them into the bowl with the seed mix.

Next, toast the cardamom seeds, cloves and cinnamon over a medium–low heat for 4–5 minutes, then add to the bowl with the other spices.

Reduce the heat to low, add the chilli powder to the pan and stir constantly with a wooden spoon to keep the powder moving, as it will turn very quickly. Toast for 4–5 minutes, until the powder is dark with a strong chilli aroma. Add to the bowl of spices.

Toast the chilli flakes in the same way, though they will take a little longer, 8–9 minutes. They are ready when they release an acrid aroma and the flakes are so dark they are almost black. Add to the bowl of spices and allow to cool completely.

Grind the spices to a fine powder then mix through the nutmeg. Store in an airtight container.

THE BASE RECIPES

(ALL THE THINGS YOU'LL NEED)

CONDIMENTS
(sambols, acharus, pickles and sauces)

I could very easily declare that condiments are the most important thing, and if you looked in my fridge at home you would see I live by this edict. I just counted, and currently we have about thirteen different things containing chilli, a shelf-and-a-half of pickles, and all the miscellaneous rest. Condiments are one of the keys to adding flavour, and a very simple way in to a country's culture. They're also a very easy way to push dishes into different countries.

One of the advantages of being in a professional kitchen is having a very excellent number of ingredients at your disposal. Pantry items are usually well stocked, but the great prize is the array of condiments, more even than you'll find in my fridge. Having these at hand makes it very easy to build new dishes. At LFS, this is where so many of our new dishes came from – we took a traditional condiment and used it in a different way.

Sometimes, I will find a new favourite sauce and become mildly obsessed by it. I will try it in all sorts of combinations; I will adjust and tweak and taste until I find where it fits best. This is how many of the recipes in this book have come about.

But first, of course, you need to have all the staples, which is what you'll find here. You probably won't have the advantage of staff and a kitchen hand, but you don't need to make everything all at once, either. Some of these are classic Sri Lankan condiments, recipes that you will also find in my previous cookbook, *Lanka Food* (LF), but that need to be repeated verbatim as they are as necessary as breathing. Others are things we have reworked using Sri Lankan ingredients. Many of them reappear in other sections of this book as a way to build new dishes, much as we do in the restaurant. Conquer this chapter and Australian–Sri Lankan food will be your plaything.

Pol sambol

MAKES APPROXIMATELY 430 G (15 OZ)

I know you're not meant to have favourites, but if I did, mine would be this one. It is truly special. This is the first sambol I learnt to make, and the one found at most meals you eat on the island. It has the perfect balance of all the flavours – sweet from coconut, sour from lime, hot from chilli and pepper with a subtle smoky depth from the Maldive fish. It exemplifies the perfect notes Sri Lankan food can hit. This recipe makes too much, but it will last a week in the fridge and is good on everything.

- 300 g (10½ oz) grated coconut
- 100 g (3½ oz) eschalots, finely diced
- 3 green bird's eye chillies, finely chopped
- 20 g (¾ oz) Maldive fish flakes, ground
- 5 g (⅕ oz) chilli powder
- 3 g (⅒ oz) freshly ground black pepper
- 3 g (⅒ oz) sweet paprika
- juice of 1–2 limes
- salt flakes

Place all the ingredients, apart from the lime juice and salt, in a bowl and firmly mix them together with one hand, using a squeezing and kneading motion. This not only combines the ingredients, it also helps release the oils from the coconut. Keep going until the texture of the sambol is almost a little sticky.

Season to taste with lime juice and a generous amount of salt, mixing and squeezing again. Serve at room temperature.

Katta sambol

MAKES APPROXIMATELY 120 G (4½ OZ)

There are so many versions of both this and lunu miris, two sambols whose names seem interchangeable depending on who you ask (I have asked a lot of people, but am still waiting on a definitive answer). It's always very hot, sometimes screamingly so. It can be cut and coarse or pounded to a paste. It sometimes has Maldive fish and sometimes doesn't. It is perfect used in the traditional way, as a chilli condiment on the side, but it can also become a seasoning when you want to spice things up. I have added it to things like radish or daikon (white radish) to make a crisp pickle-y sambol thing, it's been a base for a gotu kola (pennywort) kimchi (this was spectacularly fine), and we have also turned it into a dressing for some sambol-like salads (page 198).

- 3 long red chillies, cut into thin rounds
- 70 g (2½ oz) eschalots, finely diced
- 4 g (⅛ oz) salt flakes
- 6 g (⅕ oz) chilli flakes
- 3 g (⅒ oz) freshly ground black pepper
- juice of 1–2 limes

Using a mortar and pestle, pound the fresh chilli, eschalot, salt and chilli flakes until the mixture forms a coarse paste. It should release some liquid.

Stir through the black pepper and season to taste with lime. Serve at room temperature.

Lunu dehi mayonnaise

MAKES APPROXIMATELY 420 G (15 OZ)

This is a handy little number, tangy and sharp and good anywhere you would use a normal mayonnaise. It started life at LFS on our very first roti wrap (page 100), and pleased me both because it's delicious and because it solved a little problem we had. The pulp of the lime pickle is generally discarded, much like you do for preserved lemons, as it is intensely salty. But hiding underneath all that salinity is a powerful flavour that just needs a little taming to truly shine. Each time we made lunu dehi we would save the pulp, fish out the seeds, blend it to a paste and keep it, as I was determined to find a use for it. And here is one such use.

- 1 large whole pickled lime
- 20 g (¾ oz) Mustard (page 44)
- 3 egg yolks
- 300 ml (10 fl oz) grapeseed oil
- 20–30 ml (¾–1 fl oz) fresh lime juice
- salt flakes

To prepare your lime, separate its outer skin from the inside pulp. Finely dice the outer skin and transfer to a small mixing bowl. Remove any seeds from the pulp, then mash it finely in a mortar and pestle. Set aside.

Add the mustard, egg yolks, 10 g (⅓ oz) of the lime pulp and a little salt to the mixing bowl with the diced skin and use a whisk to combine.

Now it's just a matter of slowly drizzling in the oil, whisking as you go, to emulsify the mixture. Once all the oil is mixed in, whisk in a little lime juice and more salt to taste.

Lunu dehi

MAKES APPROXIMATELY 200 G (7 OZ)

Before making this you first need to make some lime pickle, which is a fairly simple process but does take about two months to rest. It's a good thing to do, and you'll find a recipe for this in LF, but if you don't have the patience or haven't had the foresight, never fear, just find a good Sri Lankan grocer and buy a jar. This is another beauty that will last for ages in your fridge and is good on any number of things. You'll find it among these pages with oysters (page 130) and turned into a mayonnaise, but it's also very good as the base of a salad dressing, served with cheese or added to a sandwich.

- 3 whole pickled limes
- approximately 80 g (2¾ oz) eschalots
- juice of up to 1 lime

Cut out and set aside the inner pulp from the limes and finely dice the skin. (The inner pulp can be kept, pureed and pounded and used in the mayonnaise recipe or as a very sharp and extra salty seasoning for food.)

Finely dice the eschalots. You're aiming to have equal amounts (in mass, not weight) of lime and eschalot.

Combine the pickled lime and eschalot in a bowl and mix well. The sambol should just hold together and be a little sticky rather than wet, with a nice little crunch. Season with a small amount of lime juice and serve at room temperature.

Seeni sambol

MAKES 780 G (1 LB 12 OZ)

This is a useful sambol to have on hand, and has the benefit of keeping for months, hence the larger batch size. It is basically a form of caramelised onion, complex in its flavouring thanks to the inclusion of spice, Maldive fish and sugar (seeni is Sinhalese for sugar). It's got smokiness, depth and heat, and can be slipped into any dish where you would usually find caramelised onions. Try it alongside some cheese or in a toasted cheese sandwich, next to roasted meat or livers. In fact, the list of what this matches with gets longer the more I think about it. On a potato pizza perhaps? I haven't tried that yet, but it sounds like a good idea. The key thing with this recipe is to get the onions to the right texture – cooked and caramelised, yet still holding their shape with a little crunch.

- 50 g (1¾ oz) ghee
- 1 kg (2 lb 3 oz) red onions, sliced with the grain, 2 mm (1/16 in) thick
- 24 g (⅞ oz) finely chopped garlic
- 18 g (⅔ oz) finely chopped ginger
- 8 g (¼ oz) picked curry leaves
- 40 g (1½ oz) Maldive fish flakes, ground
- 50 g (1¾ oz) jaggery, chopped
- 40 g (1½ oz) tamarind concentrate or paste
- salt flakes

SEENI SAMBOL SPICE MIX

- 7 g (¼ oz) chilli powder
- 7 g (¼ oz) salt flakes
- 3 g (1/10 oz) cinnamon stick, roughly crushed
- 3 g (1/10 oz) cardamom seeds
- 3 g (1/10 oz) black peppercorns
- 1 g (1/32 oz) whole clove (go a little under rather than over with this measure)

To prepare the seeni sambol spice mix, combine all the ingredients together and grind until smooth. This can be made ahead and then stored in an airtight container.

Over a high heat, warm your ghee in a large, wide-based shallow saucepan until it starts to smoke.

Add in a third of your onions and give them a nice stir to mix through the ghee, then let them sit undisturbed for half a minute or so. Continue in this manner, stirring and then sitting, for 4–5 minutes, until the onions have softened.

Add in another third of the onions along with the garlic, ginger and curry leaves. Continue with the stir, sit method for another 4–5 minutes.

Add in the final batch of onions and keep cooking in the same way for another 4–5 minutes.

Add in the dried fish and all of your spice mix and stir continuously to mix everything through and to make sure your onions don't catch. By this stage your onions should have softened nicely and be starting to caramelise.

Continue cooking on this high heat for 1–2 minutes before adding in the jaggery and tamarind, still stirring.

Give these final two ingredients time. The jaggery needs to melt completely and caramelise slightly and the tamarind needs to mix thoroughly. Continue cooking for 3–4 minutes, until your onion mix is dark, caramelised and looking sticky.

Remove from the heat and taste; you may need extra salt for seasoning.

Allow to cool and serve at room temperature. If you want to keep some aside in jars to store, jar it up and seal while still hot and it can be stored out of the fridge. Otherwise it will keep just as happily in a container in your fridge.

Moru chilli sambol

MAKES APPROXIMATELY 520 G (1 LB 2 OZ)

If you don't know what moru chillies are, quickly turn back to page 19. They are basically a dried chilli, but their flavour is very distinctive because of the way they are made, and their potential is far reaching. I would love to take credit for this recipe, but it was invented by my head chef, Corentin. He is rather fond of Thai food and was thinking about nam prik pao, as you do when you're a chef. He started thinking about dried chillies and then voila, this recipe was born. It's an oily chilli paste that's good for drizzling (see curried pumpkin tortellini with moru chilli sambol, page 172), for seasoning or as the base of a sauce. Use it like you would any other chilli paste – which, if you're like me, is everywhere. The main thing to focus on here is the slicing of the eschalots and garlic. They need to be very even in order to cook properly.

- 500 ml (17 fl oz) grapeseed oil (or any other neutral oil)
- 50 g (1¾ oz) moru chillies, stems removed and cut into 2 cm (¾ in) pieces (scissors are a good tool for this)
- 100 g (3½ oz) garlic cloves, finely and evenly sliced on a mandolin
- 400 g (14 oz) eschalots, finely and evenly sliced on a mandolin
- 40 g (1½ oz) jaggery, grated or finely chopped
- 15 g (½ oz) tamarind concentrate or paste

Once you have all your ingredients ready, set up your frying station. Put the oil in a wok, or saucepan, and heat it on the stove to 155°C (310°F). (When frying like this, a general rule is to always give the oil a moment to get back to this temperature in-between batches.) Have a heatproof bowl close by, on a surface that can take heat, with a fine strainer sitting in it, and a cake rack covered in paper towel nearby.

Once the oil is at the right temperature, fry the chillies, moving them around to cook evenly, for about 1–1½ minutes, until they become a darkish brown. Hold the wok carefully with both hands and pour everything directly into the strainer. This method is a lot easier and more efficient than fishing around for all of the fried bits. Tip the chilli onto the paper towel and spread it out to dry. Pour the oil back into the wok and bring it back up to temperature.

Next, fry the garlic, again moving it around to cook evenly, for about 3.5–4 minutes. You want to catch them just at the point when they are pale gold, as they will keep cooking a little after you take them off the heat. Again, strain everything and spread the garlic out along with the chillies.

Carefully transfer the oil back into the wok and heat it up again. Once it's ready, it's the eschalots' turn. This you will need to do in two batches. Cook them, stirring to ensure they cook evenly, for about 8½–9 minutes, until they are pale gold and the oil has stopped bubbling. These too will need to be strained, by which stage they will have kept cooking to a dark golden colour. Spread them on the paper towel.

Set 350 ml (12 fl oz) of the oil aside for blending, and reserve the rest for further cooking somewhere else in your life. Allow to cool slightly.

Once everything is at room temperature, place the fried bits in a Thermomix or blender along with the jaggery and tamarind. Blend until fine, slowly adding the oil back in until you have a nice smooth paste.

Store in your fridge. The oil will split out, so just make sure to re-mix it a little when you want to use the sambol. It will last longer than it takes to eat it.

Lankan chilli crunch

MAKES 750 G (1 LB 11 OZ)

Is it possible to have too many chilli condiments in your fridge? I think not. The idea for this was dreamed up by a clever chef called Pasi when he was writing a buryani menu for a series we did at LFS. He was the guest chef for the evening, but also helped with the opening of LFS (and spent many late-night post-service hours discussing the mysteries of hopper batter with me). Anyway, he said he wanted something like a Chinese chilli crunch to top his buryani. We talked ingredients and flavours, and both decided it sounded delicious. I told him we would make it, but also that we would steal the idea. I then told Corentin, who made it, and now here it is for all of us.

- 600 ml (20½ fl oz) grapeseed oil
- 5 pappadums
- 100 g (3½ oz) garlic, finely sliced on a mandolin
- 20 g (¾ oz) picked curry leaves
- 100 g (3½ oz) long red chillies, sliced into thin rounds
- 55 g (2 oz) finely chopped ginger
- 25 g (1 oz) chilli flakes
- 25 g (1 oz) chilli powder
- 10 g (⅓ oz) sweet paprika
- 20 g (¾ oz) tamarind concentrate or paste
- salt flakes, to season

Refer to the first step in the moru chilli sambol recipe (page 37) for the set-up you will need for frying.

Heat the grapeseed oil to 155°C (310°F) and fry your pappadums one by one, turning as you go, until they are crisp yet still pale. Transfer them to paper towel.

Make sure your oil is still at the right temperature and then add the garlic slices and fry, moving them around to cook evenly, for about 3.5–4 minutes. You want to catch them just at the point when they are pale gold, as they will keep cooking a little after you take them off the heat. Strain into your heatproof bowl, then spread the garlic onto the paper towel. Carefully transfer the oil back into the saucepan and bring it back up to temperature.

Gently lower your curry leaves into the oil and swish them around. They will spit and make a little mess, but there's nothing you can do about this. Fry until the oil has stopped spitting and the leaves are bright green and crisp – this will take less than a minute. Use a large, slotted spoon to scoop them out onto the paper towel.

And now it's time for the chillies. Lower these into the oil and swish them around for about 5–6 minutes, until they have softened and started to darken. Strain the chillies and place them on the rack with the other ingredients. The oil can go back into the saucepan, but leave it off the burner for a moment please.

In another heatproof bowl, combine the ginger, chilli flakes, chilli powder and paprika and mix well.

Return the oil to the heat; you want it to be sitting at about 160°C (320°F). Rest your bowl with the ginger mix on the stove next to your oil and use a ladle to pour some of the oil over the top, stirring as you go. It will sizzle and send off wafts of chilli. Keep adding the hot oil fairly swiftly until the ginger is cooked.

Let this mix sit for about half an hour to cool slightly, then add in the fried garlic, curry leaves and chillies. Coarsely crush the fried pappadums using a mortar and pestle, then add these along with the tamarind and mix well.

This will keep stored in the fridge for a long time alongside your other chilli condiments and can be used anywhere you need a little kick.

Maldive fish sambol

MAKES APPROXIMATELY 1.3 LITRES (44 FL OZ)

Chinese XO is one of the greats, and a sauce I love. Its flavour profile and ingredients are not dissimilar to what you would find in Sri Lanka, so with very few adjustments it can easily become a little bit Sri Lankan. The Maldive fish subs in for the usual scallops, the jaggery replaces white sugar and the tamarind and curry leaves are just added extras. Use it where you would use XO normally, such as in the clam dish (page 170), or do as I do for an easy dinner when real cooking seems too hard: boil some broccoli, stir in some of this sambol and eat it with brown rice.

- 300 g (10½ oz) Maldive fish flakes
- 180 g (6½ oz) small dried prawns
- 480 ml (16 fl oz) shaoxing rice wine
- 400 g (14 oz) long red chillies, cut into 2 cm (¾ in) pieces (scissors are a good tool for this)
- 120 g (4½ oz) garlic
- 40 g (1½ oz) ginger
- 1.2 litres (41 fl oz) vegetable oil
- 15 g (½ oz) picked curry leaves
- 10 g (⅓ oz) salt flakes
- 8 g (¼ oz) ground black pepper
- 40 g (1½ oz) jaggery, grated
- 25 g (1 oz) tamarind concentrate or paste

Place the Maldive fish flakes and the dried prawns into two separate bowls or containers and divide the rice wine between them, making sure they are both very well covered. They will soak up a lot of liquid, especially the prawns. Let them sit overnight.

The next day, strain off your soaked fish flakes and prawns separately, reserving the liquid. The Maldive flakes can go straight into a bowl, but the prawns will need to go into a blender. Blitz until fine and then scrape them out and add to the Maldive fish.

In the same blender (no need to wash it), add the chillies, garlic and ginger and pulse until you have a coarse paste.

Turn the paste out into a strainer to drain off any excess liquid – the less sharp or efficient your blender is, the waterier the paste can become. Set aside to strain for 30 minutes.

Pour your oil into a wok and heat over a high flame to 170°C (320°F). Add in your curry leaves and let them spit and fry a little, very closely followed by the drained chilli paste. Add the chilli paste in about three batches. Each time you add a batch, the mix should immediately sizzle and the oil will rise up. Stir well. Once the oil subsides, add in the Maldive fish flakes and prawns and continue to stir. Add in a good splash of the reserved soaking liquid.

Keep stirring until the oil is bubbling again, then turn the heat to very low. Add in the salt and pepper and let the mix cook gently for about an hour, giving it a stir every so often. Add in the jaggery and the tamarind and keep cooking for another 45 minutes.

At this stage your mixture should be nice and softened, and the oil should be beautifully red. Everything should be amalgamated and looking unctuous. Carefully have a taste (without burning your tongue) and adjust the seasoning if needed.

Remove from the heat and allow to cool, then store in the fridge.

Fried meat sambol

MAKES
1.25 LITRES
(42 FL OZ)

This Muslim dish is one of those recipes that I'd never actually eaten, but really wanted to. We discovered it in a book and it was added to the (long) list of ideas to test – and there it sat, waiting patiently for its time. Then, on a trip to SL, I discovered a market stall with an excellent array of sambols and curries. In among them was a delicious fried banana blossom sambol that got me very excited, and reminded me of the meat one that was lurking in the back of my mind. Whether ours is strictly traditional is unknown, and whether the banana blossom one was in any way similar is also a mystery, but it is very delicious. This sambol is labour-intensive and requires many steps and lots of separate frying, but it makes enough to be worth the effort. Break down the steps into separate stages for ease.

- 500 g (1 lb 2 oz) beef brisket, at room temperature
- approximately 550ml (18½ fl oz) neutral oil, for cooking and frying
- salt flakes and freshly ground pepper
- 500 g (1 lb 2 oz) brown onions, cut into even, medium slices with the grain
- 30 g (1 oz) picked curry leaves
- 10 g (⅓ oz) coriander seeds
- 15 g (½ oz) chilli flakes
- 50 g (1¾ oz) jaggery, grated or finely chopped
- 20 g (¾ oz) tamarind concentrate or paste
- lime, to serve

SPICE MIX

- 2 g (1/16 oz) black peppercorns
- 2 g (1/16 oz) cardamom seeds
- 1 g (1/32 oz) ground cinnamon
- ½ g (1/64 oz) cloves

PASTE

- 225 g (8 oz) red onions, cut into large rough dice
- 40 g (1½ oz) red chilli, cut into chunks
- 20 g (¾ oz) garlic
- 20 g (¾ oz) ginger, cut into rough pieces

For the spice mix, using a mortar and pestle, pound together the spices until fine, then set aside.

Preheat the oven to 160°C (320°F). Rub your brisket with a little of the measured oil and a good amount of salt and pepper. Place in a snug baking tray, add 250 ml (8½ fl oz) of water and cover with a sheet of baking paper. Cover this with foil, place in the oven and gently cook for 3–4 hours, until it completely gives way. Remove the foil and leave the meat until it's cool enough to handle. Once cooled, wearing gloves, break apart the meat until it is finely shredded. Lay it out on a tray and refrigerate for a few hours to dry it out a little. Once dry, add 500 ml of the oil, heat to 160°C (320°F) and shallow fry the meat until it becomes dark and crisp, being careful as it may spit quite a lot. Set aside on a wire rack to drain and cool.

Heat the same oil back up to 180°C (360°F) and shallow fry the sliced brown onions until they are an even, golden-brown colour. You may need to do this in batches. Once cooked, lay them out to drain and cool along with the fried meat.

To make the paste, combine the onion, chilli, garlic and ginger in a blender and blitz until the mixture forms a paste. Transfer to a fine strainer over a bowl and let it drain for at least an hour.

It's now time to bring it all together.

Heat 50 ml (1¾ fl oz) of oil in a large, wide-based pan over a medium-high heat. Add in the curry leaves and coriander seeds and cook, stirring, for a minute or so until they look nice and fried before adding in the drained onion paste. Give it a good few stirs and then reduce the heat to medium–low. Add the chilli flakes and the spice mix and continue stirring for 10 minutes, until the onions are well cooked.

Add in the jaggery and continue cooking, stirring occasionally, for another 5–6 minutes, until everything starts to caramelise.

Add the tamarind, mix well and then add in your fried beef and onions. Give it a good mix and cook for another 5 minutes to let everything mingle nicely before removing from the heat.

Have a little taste and season with a bit more salt if needed.

Allow to cool and store in the fridge. As you take some out to use, a little squeeze of lime is a nice way to give this a lift if needed.

NOTE Once, Corentin used some leftover mackerel to make a fish version of this. It was basically the same recipe, with the spice mix toned down a little. You could also do a jackfruit or pork version and maybe even banana blossom ...

Katta sambol
Seeni sambol
Lankan chilli crunch
Pol sambol

Maldive fish sambol
Lunu dehi mayonnaise
Moru chilli sambol
Lunu dehi
Fried meat sambol

Mustard

MAKES 1.5 LITRES (51 FL OZ)

Whoever invented mustard was clearly very clever. Many countries have their own version, including Sri Lanka, where the seeds are so abundantly used. At LFS we had our own version too, and this is it.

- 500 g (1 lb 2 oz) mustard seeds
- 700 ml (23½ fl oz) white vinegar
- 12 g (½ oz) salt flakes
- 8 g (¼ oz) black peppercorns
- 17 g (⅔ oz) garlic, roughly chopped
- 17 g (⅔ oz) ginger, roughly chopped
- 12 g (½ oz) chilli powder
- 12 g (½ oz) turmeric powder
- 8 g (¼ oz) caster (superfine) sugar

Combine the mustard seeds and vinegar in a bowl, give them a little stir and let them soak at room temperature for 12–24 hours. Strain, reserving the liquid.

Use a mortar and pestle to pound the salt and pepper until fine, then add the garlic and ginger and continue pounding until you have a paste. Set aside.

Place the mustard seeds, pounded paste and the remaining spice powders and sugar in a blender and start blending. You will need to add some of the reserved vinegar as you go, slowly, to form a paste. You don't want it to be super smooth – the mustard should look a bit finer than a wholegrain mustard.

Once you are happy with the texture, feel free to play around with the seasoning. More sugar, vinegar or salt is all okay. The mustard can be stored in the fridge or in sterilised jars for ages. Make sure to let it sit for at least a month before using.

Raita

There was a night when I was saved by the raita. I was a teenager at The India Club, a notorious London establishment, when I started to eat some sort of chilli that was so hot it burnt the edges of my lips before I even started to chew. I spent the rest of the meal whimpering slightly and delicately dabbing raita around the outside of my mouth to soothe the burn. At that stage, I knew raita to be a yoghurt and cucumber concoction, and there I thought it stopped. But as my ability to eat hotter foods has grown, so has my understanding of this helpful little side dish. Its base is always curd or yoghurt, but it can be mixed with an endless variety of vegetables, cooked or raw, tempered or slightly sweet. Raita is more of an Indian thing, and I don't remember ever eating it in Sri Lanka, but it does seem to make sense in case you need some help.

Cucumber raita

MAKES APPROXIMATELY 450 G (1 LB) / SERVES 10–12 AS PART OF A BANQUET

To me, this is the classic raita, simple and elegant and all that's needed. From this, you also get some cucumber water, which we can cleverly use somewhere else (see soda recipe, page 245).

- 1 medium telegraph (long) cucumber
- 7 g (¼ oz) salt flakes
- 300 g (10½ oz) thick Greek yoghurt
- 5 g (⅕ oz) toasted, slightly coarsely ground cumin

Using the second-finest grade on a box grater, grate the cucumber, skin and all, into a bowl. Add the salt and mix through. Transfer the cucumber mix to a fine strainer and leave to drain over a bowl for at least an hour.

Transfer the drained cucumber into a bowl and mix through the yoghurt and cumin. Serve cold.

NOTE This raita is gentle and cooling in flavour with a hint of savoury cumin.

Beetroot raita

MAKES APPROXIMATELY 450 G (1 LB)

This makes for a beautifully textured raita with an earthy, cooling flavour to it. It also has an excellent lurid colour.

- 1 large red peeled beetroot, around 200 g (7 oz)
- 5 g (⅕ oz) salt flakes, plus extra for seasoning
- 4 g (⅛ oz) ground black pepper
- 4 g (⅛ oz) ground cardamom seeds
- 250 g (9 oz) thick Greek yoghurt
- 30 g (1 oz) coconut oil
- 5 g (⅕ oz) mustard seeds
- 5 g (⅕ oz) picked curry leaves

Using the second-finest grade on a box grater, grate the beetroot into a bowl.

Add in the salt and mix through, massaging it in – you may want to use gloves for this. Once mixed, let the beetroot sit for an hour before squeezing all the moisture out (again with the gloves ...).

Place the beetroot in a bowl and mix through the black pepper, cardamom and yoghurt. Transfer the raita to a serving dish – something shallow and a bit wide is perfect. Set aside.

Warm a small frying pan over a medium heat then add the coconut oil. Once the oil just starts to shimmer from heat, add in the mustard seeds and curry leaves. Stir until the mustard seeds are popping and the curry leaves are fried and crisp, then remove from the heat and spoon over your raita. Season with a sprinkle of salt flakes and serve. The raita should still be a little cold when you serve it, despite the hot temper on top.

Pistachio, almond, cardamom and kithul raita

MAKES APPROXIMATELY 500G (1 LB 2 OZ)

If you're looking for a fragrant, subtly sweet raita, as one does, then this is for you. It feels special. Pair it with some saffron-scented rice and you'll feel like you should be floating around in a sari on a balmy tropical evening with a sitar playing in the background.

- 100 g (3½ oz) whole raw pistachios
- 100 g (3½ oz) whole raw almonds, skin on
- 250 g (9 oz) thick Greek yoghurt
- 6 g (⅕ oz) salt flakes
- 4 g (⅛ oz) ground cardamom
- 2 g (1⁄16 oz) ground black pepper
- 60 ml (2 fl oz) kithul

Preheat the oven to 150°C (300°F). Lay your nuts out separately on small trays and lightly roast them. Give them a couple of jiggles as they cook to make sure they roast evenly. The pistachios will take about 10 minutes, the almonds 15 minutes. Set aside until completely cooled.

Once cooled, use a mortar and pestle to coarsely grind the nuts in batches. You just want to break them up, you don't want them powdery. Once the nuts are broken up, transfer them to a mixing bowl.

Thoroughly mix in the yoghurt, salt and spices and transfer to a serving dish. To finish, drizzle the kithul on top.

Pistachio, almond, cardamon and kithul raita

Cucumber raita

Beetroot raita

Pineapple chutney
Karkalla acharu
Pickled beetroot
Pickled green chillies
Pickled cherries
Pickled mustard seeds
Jackfruit acharu

Pickles and acharu

Is an acharu (achcharu/achar/etc ...) a pickle by another name? Kind of, and not really. However, acharus and pickles do live in the same territory, as both are fresh produce that has been salted or vinegared or both to preserve the food and make it taste good. The following recipes are more pickle-like in their methods, though still Lankan in flavour. Whatever you would like to call them, they are an excellent thing to have on hand. Their greatest beauty is that they catch the bounty of nature in its excess to store for later, but also, they're such an easy way to liven things up it almost feels like cheating. There are very few places a pickle isn't welcome, although I was recently sternly admonished and told to change a planned menu as there are rules. A vegetable acharu should only be eaten as an accompaniment to a rice and curry meal and a fruit acharu should only be served as a snack. Perhaps traditionally this is so, but you can imagine my thoughts on this. Add it to a cocktail (see acharu martini, page 256) to start you off, snack on them pre-dinner to get the appetite flowing, slip them into a toasted sandwich (see jaffles, pages 91–2), or use them in a salad or on the side to provide respite among rich flavours.

Acharu liquor

MAKES 500 ML (17 FL OZ) PICKLE LIQUOR

This base recipe is an easy way to pickle almost anything and infuse it with a little Lankan flavour. Add more salt if you intend to keep something for a long time – this is best on more hardy produce – or pull back if you are doing a quick pickle that you want to use straight away. The amount of sugar can be adjusted to taste.

- 3 g (⅒ oz) black peppercorns
- 4 g (⅛ oz) mustard seeds
- 190 ml (6½ fl oz) cider vinegar
- 38 g (1½ oz) caster (superfine) sugar
- 11 g (⅓ oz) cooking salt
- 6 g (⅕ oz) chilli powder
- 6 g (⅕ oz) turmeric powder

Place the peppercorns and mustard seeds in a pan over a low heat and gently toast for 2–3 minutes. Use a mortar and pestle to coarsely grind the peppercorns and mustard seeds.

Tip the pepper mix into a large saucepan and add the remaining ingredients, along with 300 ml (10 fl oz) of water. Place over a medium heat and slowly bring to a boil. Simmer for 5 minutes to allow the flavours time to mingle, then remove from the heat and set aside.

Persimmon acharu

MAKES APPROXIMATELY 400 G (14 OZ)

This is a delicious fruit with two main varieties and a very short season. There is the squishy one, which needs to be eaten fully ripe, when it becomes delicious and jammy, and the other variety, fuyu, which is eaten when firm. This is the one we are going to use. They make a quick pickle with a lovely crunch and a delicately sweet and fragrant flavour.

- 2 firm fuyu persimmons
- 1 batch Acharu liquor (page 49), cold
- salt flakes
- a gentle extra virgin olive oil

Using a mandolin, slice the persimmons from the base to the top into 5 mm (⅛ in) rounds and place in a mixing bowl.

Pour over the acharu liquor and gently mix, ensuring the fruit is fully immersed. Transfer it into the fridge.

To serve, pull the persimmon out of the pickle liquor, arrange it nicely on a dish and let it come to room temperature. Spoon over some of the liquid, then season lightly with some salt flakes and a generous drizzle of olive oil.

Given the delicate nature of the persimmon, this pickle will keep for about a week before it starts losing the flavour of the fruit.

Jackfruit acharu

MAKES – IT DEPENDS, HOW BIG IS YOUR FRUIT?

This is an acharu I would always have on the menu if it weren't for its many obstacles. Jackfruit isn't always in season, and it's a lengthy, sticky and messy process to prepare, with a lot of waste, and is therefore costly in terms of wages. Plus, they are expensive to buy and are often very large, which can be intimidating. This is a labour of love, but my friends, it is worth it.

- 320 ml (11 fl oz) warm Acharu liquor (page 49), per 500 g (1 lb 2 oz) of prepared fruit
- salt flakes
- a gentle extra virgin olive oil

For this recipe you will need to learn how to grapple a jackfruit. Use this photo guide to help you.

Essentially, you want to end up with the soft flesh of the fruit that looks pod-like. You then remove the hard internal seed from each pod, either by popping it out or gently slitting open an edge to remove. The seeds can be kept and dried and used elsewhere (see online for recipes).

Once your fruit is prepped, place it into a mixing bowl and pour the warm acharu liquor over the top. Let it sit until it reaches room temperature and then store in the fridge overnight.

The pickle will last at its best for up to 7 days.

To serve, pull out as much of the pickle as you want and allow it to come to room temperature. Spoon over a bit of the liquor and season lightly with some salt flakes and a generous drizzle of olive oil.

Karkalla acharu

MAKES APPROXIMATELY 400 G (14 OZ)

This is a native Australian sea succulent also known as beach banana (because it kind of looks like a banana, and it lives by the ocean) or pigface. Its beauty lives in its briny flavour and its texture, which combines a crunchy exterior and a jelly-like centre. It is delicious raw, but also very good gently pickled, as here. Another oceanic ingredient in this same realm is samphire, which can also be made using the method below and is equally delicious.

- 400 g (14 oz) karkalla
- 1 batch Acharu liquor (page 49), at room temperature
- salt flakes
- a gentle extra virgin olive oil

To prepare your karkalla, pick through it and gently break the pieces apart so you have just small bunches, discarding any bits that aren't looking super fresh. Place the karkalla into a mixing bowl.

Pour over the acharu liquor and gently mix, ensuring the karkalla is fully immersed. Let it sit at room temperature for an hour or so before using. This acharu is best used on the day you make it. It will last in the fridge for a few days, but you will lose a bit of the subtlety of the karkalla's flavour.

To serve, spoon over a bit of the liquor and season lightly with some salt flakes and a generous drizzle of olive oil. If you have kept it in the fridge, allow it to come to room temperature before serving.

Pickled beetroot

MAKES APPROXIMATELY 600 G (1 LB 5 OZ)

This is a really simple way of dealing with beetroots that doesn't involve any cooking. It makes for a lovely, textured pickle.

- 3 medium red beetroot, around 550 g (1 lb 3 oz)
- 5 g (⅕ oz) cooking salt
- 1 batch Acharu liquor (page 49), hot off the stove
- salt flakes
- a gentle extra virgin olive oil

Wearing disposable gloves, peel your beetroots and then, using a mandolin, slice them from the base to the top into even 2 mm (1⁄16 in) rounds and place in a mixing bowl. Massage in the cooking salt and let the beetroots sit for an hour.

Squeeze out any liquid and discard before returning the beetroot to the bowl.

Pour over the acharu liquor and gently mix, ensuring the beetroot is fully immersed. Let it sit at room temperature until the liquor has completely cooled before transferring to the fridge to sit overnight.

The pickle will last at its best for up to 2 weeks.

To serve, pull out as much of the pickle as you want and allow it to come to room temperature. Spoon over a bit of the liquor and season lightly with some salt flakes and a generous drizzle of olive oil.

Pickled cherries

MAKES 1 LARGE JAR

This is an old Berta recipe, and one that became a bit of a yearly Christmas tradition. As it turns out, a lot of the spices fit neatly under the umbrella of Sri Lankan flavours and allowed me to seamlessly carry on with it at LFS.

- 1 kg (2 lb 3 oz) cherries
- 800 ml (27 fl oz) red wine vinegar
- 225 g (8 oz) caster (superfine) sugar
- 75 g (2¾ oz) cooking salt
- 10 g (⅓ oz) mustard seeds
- 3 g (⅒ oz) black peppercorns
- 1 cinnamon stick
- 3 cloves
- 5 cardamom pods
- 3 fresh bay leaves
- 5 g (⅕ oz) picked curry leaves

Gently wash the cherries, leaving the stalks attached, then place them in a colander to drain. One by one, take each cherry and lightly score the underside with a small slash.

To make the pickle liquor, place all remaining ingredients except the curry leaves in a medium saucepan along with 400 ml (13½ fl oz) of water and bring to a boil over a high heat. Reduce to a simmer and continue cooking for another 5 minutes, then remove from the heat and throw in the curry leaves.

Place your cherries in a sterilised jar and pour over the hot pickle liquor until it reaches almost to the top, making sure all the spices find their way in. Give the jar a good few taps on the bench to remove any air bubbles. Cut out a round of baking paper to fit snugly over the top of the cherries and press down to submerge them. You may lose some liquor, so be sure to re-top up to make sure all the cherries are submerged.

Seal the lid tightly, write the date on the top and place it somewhere darkish. The cherries need to sit for about 3 months before use. Once you have opened the jar, store the remaining cherries in the fridge, where they should last for another few months.

NOTE Because of the delicate nature of cherries, this pickle will only last at its best for just over a year.

Pickled green chillies

MAKES 1 LARGE JAR

I always like to have a pickled green chilli on hand; it's like a security blanket for me. I think these too are an old Berta recipe, but pickled green chillies are found all over the world, and rightly so – they are a delicious morsel and good for everything.

- 500 g (1 lb 2 oz) long green chillies
- 600 ml (20½ fl oz) cider vinegar
- 50 g (1¾ oz) dark brown sugar
- 27 g (1 oz) cooking salt

Wash your chillies and prepare a sterilised jar. You want the chillies to fit snugly, but once they have sat in the liquor they will shrink quite a lot, so you will probably need a smaller jar than you suspect. Trial and error is the only way forward here.

Place the green chillies in a mixing bowl. To make the pickling liquor, combine the remaining ingredients with 600 ml (20½ fl oz) of water in a medium saucepan and bring to a boil over a high heat. Remove from the heat and allow to cool to room temperature.

Once cooled, pour the liquor over the chillies and leave to sit for about 2 hours.

Using tongs, carefully arrange the chillies in the jar – they should fit snugly. Pour over the pickle liquor until it reaches the top, then give the jar a good few taps on the bench to remove any air bubbles. Cut out a round of baking paper to fit snugly over the top of the chillies and press down to submerge them. You may lose some liquor, so be sure to re-top up to make sure all the chillies are submerged.

Let the chillies sit for about 2 months before using. Once you have opened the jar, store the remaining chillies in the fridge, where they will last for a good couple of months.

Pickled mustard seeds

MAKES 330 ML (11 FL OZ)

Using tempered mustard seeds to finish a dish is common in Sri Lanka and India, and having a pickled version kind of works in the same vein. It's a little extra pop of flavour, and gives a lift to salads, braised dishes, soups or lentils. These are also good with cured meats (see buffalo herder, page 120).

- 520 ml (17½ fl oz) cider vinegar
- 50 g (1¾ oz) caster (superfine) sugar
- 8 g (¼ oz) cooking salt
- 150 g (5½ oz) mustard seeds

Combine all ingredients with 500 ml (17 fl oz) of water in a medium saucepan and bring to a boil over a medium heat. Turn the heat down and simmer gently for about 80 minutes, until the mustard seeds are soft, puffy and plump.

While still hot, pour everything into a sterilised jar and seal. The mustard seeds need to sit for about a month before they are ready to use. Once ready, the mustard seeds can be kept in the fridge, and will last for longer than I've ever tested.

Date and tamarind chutney

MAKES 300 G (10½ OZ)

Chutneys were a bit thin on the ground at LFS, mostly because their sweet fruitiness wasn't high on my list of food cravings. I slowly came around, however, and conceded that there was an appropriate place for them. I started with this Lankan classic. On my first go I made an overcomplicated version involving too many ingredients, resulting in a weirdly textured mess with flavours that didn't really make sense. I attempted to salvage it a few times, but it just got more confusing, so I gave up. Corentin stepped in and made this version which, you'll be pleased to know, is simple and delicious.

- 150 g (5½ oz) block of tamarind
- 55 g (2 oz) deseeded dates
- 90 g (3 oz) jaggery, grated or finely chopped
- 2.7 g (1⁄10 oz) ground ginger powder
- 2 g (1⁄16 oz) cumin seeds, toasted and finely ground
- 1 g (1⁄32 oz) salt flakes

Break up the block of tamarind, place it in a heatproof bowl along with the dates and pour over 500 ml (17 fl oz) of boiling water. Let it sit for about 30 minutes to rehydrate, then use the back of a spoon to break it up and release the pulp.

Use a fine strainer over a medium saucepan to sieve the paste into the pan. Press it through to release as much of the pulp as possible.

Add the rest of the ingredients to the saucepan, mix well and place over a low heat. Gently cook the chutney, stirring occasionally for 1 hour, until it has a nice thick, smooth and glossy texture. Remove from the heat.

The chutney can be stored at room temperature in a sterilised jar or in the fridge for a long time.

Pineapple chutney

MAKES 450 G (1 LB)

The flavour of this is all about the pineapple, with a little extra sweetness from the jaggery, which gives a hint of smoke alongside the bitterness from cooking it down to a dark caramel. This is a handy little condiment, good in a jaffle with ham and cheese, added to your next burger with beetroot to be properly Australian, served next to some cheese or cured meats, or as a condiment to serve with cooked meats for a bit of extra smoky sweet flavour.

- 1 small sweet pineapple, around 1 kg (2 lb 3 oz)
- 200 g (7 oz) jaggery, chopped
- 6 g (1/5 oz) chilli powder
- 5 g (1/5 oz) salt flakes
- 3 g (1/10 oz) ground black pepper
- 2 g (1/16 oz) cardamom seeds
- 1 whole star anise

Peel your pineapple. Cut half into rough chunks and blend it until you have a smooth paste. Cut the other half into small dice. There is no need to discard the core unless it is particularly woody, in which case you can discard (but note that the recipe ratios may be out a little).

Place all the pineapple along with the remaining ingredients into a heavy-based medium saucepan and mix well. Place the saucepan over a high heat, bring the mix to a boil and then reduce the temperature to a gentle simmer.

Cook, stirring occasionally, for about 30 minutes, until the mix is sticky and dark. Have a little taste and adjust your seasoning as needed.

Eat immediately, or transfer to a sterilised jar to store. Serve at room temperature.

NOTE This chutney should be hot and sticky, the sweetness tempered by a darker charred flavour. You want to be able to taste all the spices, particularly the black pepper.

Butters

At first glance, flavoured butter doesn't seem to follow in the tradition of Sri Lankan cooking, but if you view it as a version of a temper, it does make sense. Regardless, it's just another tool for adding an extra boost of flavour, and fat. Compound butters are used regularly in restaurants, in amounts that would be slightly terrifying to the normal human. These recipes are for big batches that will keep, so you can use them sparingly if you must, or make like a chef, add with gay abandon and discover one of the secrets to why restaurant food tastes so good.

Curry leaf butter

MAKES APPROXIMATELY 1 KG (2 LB 3 OZ)

I first came across curry leaf butter in the kitchen at Vulcans, a singular restaurant in Sydney's Blue Mountains that was an early yet integral part of my cooking journey, way before I ever imagined myself in a kitchen – in fact, I was still a teenager when it opened. There was some sort of roasted pumpkin dish on the menu and it was drizzled with curry leaf butter, maybe with some mustard seeds too, much like a classic Indian temper. I can't tell you anything else about it, but that particular flavour combination implanted itself in my early food memory and is one I still come back to. There is something about sweet pumpkin with savoury curry leaf that drives me wild. Once I had my own kitchen, curry leaf butter quickly appeared and was used wherever I could slip it in. Two perfect uses for it are in a bacon sandwich – just make your perfect version of this classic, but be sure to add excessive curry leaf butter and lots of black pepper – and an early Berta lunch special of a toasted mozzarella, cheddar and curry leaf butter sandwich (page 91).

1 kg (2 lb 3 oz) cold unsalted butter, diced

90 g (3 oz) picked curry leaves

Place the diced butter and curry leaves in a saucepan over a gentle heat. Let the butter slowly melt and heat, and the curry leaves cook.

Once the curry leaves are crisp – this should take about 15 minutes – remove from the heat and allow to cool.

Pass the mix through a fine sieve in a large bowl, making sure to squeeze out as much fat as you can. Let the butter cool in the fridge until it solidifies slightly again.

Place the butter into a Thermomix or blender and blitz until you have a homogenised butter. This will last in the fridge for an age, and even longer in the freezer.

Hot butter

MAKES APPROXIMATELY 1 KG (2 LB 3 OZ)

Hot butter cuttlefish (page 144), a famed Lankan dish, was always going to be on the LFS menu. It's cooked with butter, obviously, and the traditional version has relatively few other ingredients. Somehow as I was testing this dish, I managed to make a version that was slightly more complicated, as I am wont to do, and much more spice heavy. So, in a bid for consistency, we mixed everything together to make this super-fiery butter. It very quickly became a kitchen snack, a scoop of it atop dhal, which led to a jaffle (page 92) and from there, there was no stopping it. Among other things, we've used it to stir-fry mushrooms, corn and padron peppers, and it has become a sauce for fried fish wings (page 146) and crab (page 161). It's the butter that can do anything.

45 g (1½ oz) salt flakes

30 g (1 oz) chilli flakes

30 g (1 oz) coriander seeds

30 g (1 oz) black peppercorns

55 g (2 oz) chilli powder

10 g (¼ oz) turmeric powder

12 g (½ oz) picked curry leaves

900 g (2 lb) unsalted butter, diced and at room temperature

Combine the salt, chilli flakes, coriander seeds and peppercorns in a blender and blitz until fine.

Add the remaining ingredients to the blender and blitz until the butter is light and fluffy. The butter will last in the fridge for an age, and even longer in the freezer.

Vadouvan butter

MAKES APPROXIMATELY 1.5–1.6 KG (3 LB 5 OZ–3½ LB) BUTTER

Vadouvan is a particular spice mix that was developed by French colonists in South India adapting a masala to suit their European palates. It is a complex, fragrant and aromatic number with little to no chilli and a beautiful gentle sweetness. I think my first encounter with it was at a French restaurant, where it was served with seared livers and a generous smattering of extra fried curry leaves. The dish immediately won my heart. So, of course, somewhere along the line we created our version with the addition of orange peel, which was inspired by something – I'm not sure what. The sweet citrus is a very happy friend to curry leaves, both of which are from the same family, and it seems to work beautifully. It works anywhere you want to add butter with more flavour, simply tossed through some pasta, for example, but it is particularly fine served with most types of seafood. There are a lot of ingredients in this recipe – don't be scared, just think of it as a slightly complicated curry powder.

- 1 kg (2 lb 3 oz) cold unsalted butter, diced
- 600 g (1 lb 5 oz) eschalots, finely sliced on a mandolin
- 50 g (1¾ oz) garlic, finely sliced on a mandolin
- 50 g (1¾ oz) ginger, finely sliced on a mandolin
- 6 g (⅕ oz) picked curry leaves
- skin of 1 large orange, white pith removed, julienned
- 10 g (⅓ oz) turmeric powder
- 6 g (⅕ oz) coriander seeds
- 3 g (⅒ oz) cumin seeds
- 2 g (1⁄16 oz) black peppercorns
- 2 g (1⁄16 oz) fenugreek
- 2 g (1⁄16 oz) fennel seeds
- 2 g (1⁄16 oz) cardamom seeds
- 1 g (1⁄32 oz) cloves
- 20 g (¾ oz) cooking salt

Put the butter into a large saucepan and, as you prepare each ingredient, throw it on top, ensuring all of the fresh ingredients are sliced evenly. Once everything is in the saucepan, place it over a low heat.

Once the butter melts, continue cooking until the mixture reaches 80°C (175°F). Keep it at this temperature, stirring occasionally, for about 30 minutes. Remove from the heat and allow to cool completely.

Once cooled, blend in a Thermomix or blender until you have a homogenised butter. The butter will last in the fridge for an age, and even longer in the freezer.

Fermented
chilli powder
Fermented
chilli mayonnaise
Fermented
chilli sauce

Fermented chilli

Base, sauce, powder and mayonnaise

We were always going to have a chilli sauce on the menu at LFS but, somehow, we were close to opening and still didn't have a version that we'd tested. A slight amount of desperation, a surplus of bird's eye chillies and a panicked phone call to my partner Mat for advice (who I call Muu, as that was his nickname in the kitchen where we first met, many moons ago) combined to give us our sauce, which turned out to be too stupidly hot. We tried again, sans bird's eyes, and were very happy. The fermentation works on ratios, which means you can use whatever chillies you like – add in some extra hot ones if you are feeling daring, or slip in some red capsicum (bell pepper) to dial down the heat. It's a very adaptable recipe.

We go for long red chillies with garlic in the base ferment, and then adjust for consistency using a sugar syrup. The thick sugar syrup gives the sauce some body, and a little sweet balance with the chilli flakes, which we use in varying amounts, is our way of keeping the heat consistent. Where you leave this to ferment will have a big impact on how quickly it's ready – the warmer it is the faster it goes. This recipe says to leave it for a week, but the best way to be sure is to smell your ferment daily and decide when you think it's ready. Use common sense and your nose as a guide. If it smells good to you, it should taste good. You can use the fermented chilli base straight up. Simply transfer it to the fridge, skipping the blending step, covered with a little oil, and use as you would any other chilli condiment. Or, move straight to the sauce recipe.

Fermented chilli sauce

MAKES APPROXIMATELY 600 ML (20½ FL OZ) SAUCE

The finished result here will vary depending on you and your chillies. The type of chilli used, and the season they're grown in will have the greatest impact on the heat and flavour of the sauce. But how powerful your blender is, the place you choose to ferment your sauce and the amount of sugar syrup you use will also play a part. That's when you get to decide things for yourself. Taste the chilli base and if you don't think it's hot enough, perhaps add extra flakes into the syrup at the end. Adjust how long you leave it to ferment, and add more or less sugar to suit your own palate. You will end up with your very own version of a perfect chilli sauce that's good on everything.

- 500 g (1 lb 2 oz) long red chillies
- 65 g (2¼ oz) garlic cloves
- 23 g (⅞ oz) cooking salt
- 82 g (2¾ oz) caster (superfine) sugar
- 20 ml (¾ fl oz) cider vinegar, plus extra for seasoning
- 20 g (¾ oz) chilli flakes

Using kitchen scissors, cut the chillies into 1 cm (½ in) chunks, discarding the stems. Set aside.

In batches, blend the fresh chilli, garlic, salt and 12 g (½ oz) of the sugar to a coarse paste. Transfer the mixture to a container with a lid and set it aside at room temperature to ferment. Leave to sit for about a week (but really, anywhere between 3–14 days).

Once the ferment is ready, re-blend it with the vinegar as finely as you can. Pass this pulp through a fine strainer or drum sieve, pressing it through quite forcefully to get out as much pulpy liquid as you can. Set aside the remains in the sieve and use it to make the fermented chilli powder (recipe opposite).

Meanwhile, make the sugar syrup. Place the remaining caster sugar in a small saucepan with 20 ml (¾ fl oz) of water and let it come to a boil before adding the chilli flakes. Let the syrup simmer for 5 minutes, then cool to room temperature before straining out the flakes.

Slowly whisk the sugar syrup into the strained chilli pulp, tasting as you go – you may not need to add it all in. Use just enough to ensure your sauce has a nice flavour and a good, thick consistency. If you've got the right consistency but your sauce is a little too sweet, adjust with a little extra vinegar. Fiddle around until you are happy.

Store your chilli sauce in a sterilised bottle at room temperature or keep it in the fridge. Either way, it lasts a very long time.

Fermented chilli powder

The strained pulp leftovers from making the chilli sauce will look like a dry, seedy paste that could easily be thrown away, but wait, it can have purpose. Cover a large baking tray with baking paper and evenly spread the paste over it in a thin layer. Place the tray into an oven with only the pilot light on and leave it overnight to dry completely. Once dry, blend until fine, place in a jar and boast that you've got your own house-made chilli powder. It will be much more mellow than a normal chilli powder, with a sweet, slightly fermented undertone. It's excellent for seasoning when you only want a subtle kick, or as a substitute for hot chilli powder when you want to tone things down a bit.

Fermented chilli mayonnaise

Finally, add some of your chilli sauce to mayonnaise, to bring out the sweetness in the chilli. Again, you get all the flavour but only a subtle heat. Make a base mayonnaise as you would normally – make sure it's a thick one – then fold in chilli sauce, to taste, at the end. Be careful though – if you add too much, you will end up with a runny mayonnaise. Finish with a flourish of fermented chilli powder for extra effect.

TO START

(OR END)

THE DAY

BREAKFASTS, BUNS AND SANDWICHES

My first proper trip to Sri Lanka was full of food revelations, but the greatest was the excellent breakfasts. There were hoppers, curries, spicy sambols, rice-based dishes and an excellent array of tropical fruit cut just so, to cleanse. I discovered a morning hunger in me that I didn't know existed. This was holiday mode though, a time when hotel buffets are at your disposal, as well as long, slow leisurely starts to the day and the bonus of knowing that all that cooking and cleaning is someone else's problem. But even the quick mid-week breakfasts still have that savoury, spicy element to them, like the great go-to of kade paan with some dhal and a bit of pol sambol – quite different to growing up in Australia, when a bowl of (usually) sweet cereal or muesli is the fast option.

There is definitely a stark contrast between what appears at the breakfast table in Australia compared to most of Asia, and I am firmly in the latter camp. I love a savoury start to the day, so a little bit of hot and spicy suits me very nicely, thank you. Rice for breakfast makes sense to me, as does a soup, a pickle or anything spiced. I do understand that not everyone wants breakfast at all, and even if they do, the thought of something strongly flavoured can be too much to stomach at that hour. Luckily though, things seemingly made for breakfast are good at any time of the day (including cornflakes, which I think are an excellent just-before-bed snack).

The recipes here are savoury, breakfast-type things, all of which can be embraced at any time, from your first morning repast until the end of the day. We have a few Sri Lankan classics that have been tweaked with added flavours, and we also have a whole range of buns and sandwich-type things, including that excellent Australian invention, the jaffle – a toasted sandwich that encases its filling, making it the perfect vessel to fill with leftovers, curry being a particularly excellent option. If I may be so bold to declare, a curry jaffle could be the ultimate in Australian–Sri Lankan fusion.

Scrambled eggs

SERVES 2

Sadly, I didn't grow up eating proper Sri Lankan breakfasts, but this little number often made an appearance. It's based on my mum Chaz's version of a home-style dish – apparently her brother, my uncle Dazzy, does a similar thing but adds Maldive fish, which I have never tried but fully endorse. These eggs are super savoury and slot in nicely if you want to do a Western breakfast thingy with bacon and roast tomatoes. Or you could be more Sri Lankan and serve this with lingus (page 88), dhal (page 212) and kade paan (page 106). Whichever way you go, this is a very easy way to spice up ordinary eggs, and it's also an excellent bridge, nudging you closer to the full Lanky way of starting the day with curries galore.

- 6 eggs
- 1 g (1⁄32 oz) chilli powder
- 30 g (1⁄2 oz) ghee
- 3 g (1⁄10 oz) picked curry leaves
- 2 g (1⁄16 oz) mustard seeds
- 1 small red onion, thinly sliced with the grain
- 1 long green chilli, thinly sliced
- salt flakes and freshly ground black pepper

Break your eggs into a mixing bowl, add the chilli powder and whisk well, making sure the powder doesn't go clumpy, then set aside.

Place a large frying pan over a medium–high heat and add your ghee. Once the ghee melts and starts to shimmer, add in the curry leaves and mustard seeds. There will be some spitting.

Using a heatproof spatula, mix this around until the leaves look fried, just for a moment, then add in the onion and chilli and season well. Cook, stirring often, for another 3–4 minutes, until the onion starts to caramelise a little.

Once you are happy with the onion, turn the heat to high and pour the whisked eggs into the pan. Let the mixture sit for a few moments, then drag your spatula through the mix from the bottom to the top of the pan. Keep cooking in this manner, kind of folding the eggs rather than mixing them, to your desired doneness – I like mine a little soft. Transfer to plates and serve immediately.

Sri Lankan omelette

SERVES 1

While this is a very easy recipe, it is a bit of a Lankan staple that I feel deserves its spot here. It often has other additions, most of which I'm uninterested in, including tomato, which I'll accept, capsicum, which I won't, and other variations like chilli powder and coconut instead of cow's milk. I suppose it's the curry leaves that make it Sri Lankan, but really, it's the texture that makes it so different from a classic French omelette with its soft and runny ways. Instead, what we have here is thin, cooked through and a bit more like a pancake. It makes for a very good filling in between kade paan (page 106) with lashings of butter, perfect to eat on the go in a tuk-tuk on a Lankan adventure. I have seen recipes for an omelette curry using this as the base, which I am yet to attempt but would really like to. Perhaps for the next book ...

- 30 g (1 oz) ghee
- ¼ small red onion, cut into medium dice
- 1–2 small green chillies, thinly sliced
- 2 g (1/16 oz) picked curry leaves, finely sliced
- 3 eggs
- 40 ml (1¼ oz) full cream (whole) milk
- salt flakes and freshly ground black pepper

Warm an omelette-sized frying pan (I would go about 20 cm/7 in) over a medium heat. Add in the ghee, and once the ghee is shimmering add the onion, chilli and curry leaves and stir to cook. Keep stirring for about 5 minutes, until the onion has softened and starts to go translucent.

While the onion is cooking, whisk the eggs and milk in a bowl and season with salt and pepper. Turn the heat to low and spread the cooked onion mix evenly around the pan before pouring in the egg mixture. Let it sit, cooking gently until cooked through. This should take about 5 minutes plus a little extra time for it to rest in the pan off the heat. There is no need to flip it. If you are Sri Lankan, feel free to cook it a little longer; less so if you happen to be French ...

Turn the omelette onto a plate and eat it while hot. Toast is a good accompaniment, and even better if it's kade paan.

HOW TO COOK FRIED EGGS IN A WOK

(a method of frying eggs learnt at Billy Kwong)

This method can seem slightly ridiculous in a home setting due to the excessive amount of oil used, but the result is truly delicious. If done correctly, the whites become lacy and crisp while the yolks are perfectly runny and oozy. It also looks very impressive. There is a bit of a technique to getting it right, but with a bit of practice you'll soon have it down. You can adapt this method using a wide-based frying pan, but a wok is best as the shape provides more surface area for the amount of oil used, which leaves room to spread out the eggs if you're cooking in batches. Plus, it allows you to do the flicky thing with your spatula. Here's how ...

To prepare

EGGS

Use cold ones.

Have them cracked into a bowl ready to go.

Don't use eggs with a broken yolk – for some reason, when broken yolks hit the oil they spit very dramatically. This is because fatty things spit in hot oil. I'm not really sure why, though, as I am not a scientist.

Always be gentle when moving the cooked eggs around, as the yolks can easily break, run out of the base and spit (see above).

Don't crowd the wok. Most domestic woks will take four eggs at the most.

Line a wire rack with paper towel for draining and keep this close at hand – but not so close that the paper towel is in danger of catching fire (something I may have done once or twice).

NOTE Safety first: make sure your wok is very stable and, once the oil heats up, always keep one hand on the handle to avoid tipping.

Now, to begin

Fill your wok up two-thirds with a neutral oil and heat to 170°C (340°F).

Have one hand on the wok handle, the other holding a flexible metal spatula backwards.

Pour the eggs into the middle of the wok. They should fall to the bottom and then quickly spring up to the surface with the whites spreading out.

Let them sit there for about 5 seconds, allowing the bottom to set so you don't break the yolks (again, danger, see previous page).

Using the spatula at the outer edges of the egg, flick the hot oil over the top of the eggs continuously until the entire top becomes a beautiful golden brown.

Flip your spatula and carefully scoop up the eggs. Lean them against the side of the wok to drain the oil, then carefully transfer to your wire rack.

Let the eggs sit for a few seconds to drain off the excess oil before transferring to your preferred serving dish.

TIMES

1 egg takes about 40 seconds to 1 minute to cook in total (if you are cooking one egg at a time, only fill your wok halfway with oil).

4 eggs take about 1½ minutes to cook in total.

2 and 3 eggs take somewhere in between.

HEAT

If you are doing more than one batch, allow your oil to reheat between each go.

If the oil is too hot, the whites will burn or cook too fast for the yolks to heat enough.

If the oil is not hot enough the eggs will get a bit flabby and oily, and the yolks will overcook before the whites get crispy enough.

Fried eggs with kiri hodi and moru chilli crumb

SERVES 2

There was an egg dish on the menu at Billy Kwong, which was a great example of something for dinner that would be equally good for breakfast, the eggs fried using the wok method (see pages 73–5). It was a perfect dish: the eggs dressed with oyster and chilli sauce, coriander, shallots and fresh chilli, offering a mix of textures and flavours. It was a rich number, made even more decadent when cooked with duck eggs, as it originally was. And then, in Sri Lanka, one of the great breakfasts (or easy dinners) is kiri hodi (page 205), a gentle, runny coconut milk curry, almost like a sauce, often boiled eggs bobbing around in it, served with string hoppers, a delicate steamed rice flour pancake, and a fiery sambol on the side. Cross these two things and you get this perfect hybrid breakfast (or dinner), the crisp whites mimicking the lacy string hoppers and the yolks breaking into the curry sauce, creating a delicious puddle.

- 150 ml (5 fl oz) Kiri hodi (page 205)
- vegetable oil, for frying
- 4 eggs
- coriander (cilantro) leaves, to garnish
- toast or roti, to serve

MORU CHILLI CRUMB

- 2 g (1/16 oz) white peppercorns
- 1 g (3/32 oz) salt flakes
- 4 fried moru chillies, cut into pieces

For the moru chilli crumb, use a mortar and pestle to grind the pepper and salt until coarse. Add in the moru chillies and continue grinding until the pepper is mostly fine and the chillies are broken up into small pieces. Set aside.

Warm up the kiri hodi and have it ready to serve.

Cook your eggs using the wok frying method (see pages 73–5) then transfer them to a shallow bowl.

Using kitchen scissors or the tip of a sharp knife, cut into the yolks so they run a little.

Ladle on the kiri hodi, sprinkle with the moru chilli crumb and top with coriander. Serve immediately with toast or roti.

Pumpkin kola kanda

SERVES 4–6

Kola kanda is a murky green Lankan rice porridge that is sometimes thick and sometimes a bit runnier. It is said to be healthful, as it's made with any number of bitter and wild leaves: kola being Sinhalese for (green) leaves, kanda being a type of porridge. This version uses pumpkin instead of greens, which means it is slightly misnamed (pumpkin green leaf porridge?) but it's kind of the same idea. This makes a hearty breakfast, and good if you have a glut of pumpkins and are sick of making plain old soup. It's delicious as is, but you can fluff it up with condiments as you would a congee. I add roti on the side, toasted or cut into strips and fried, and serve it with spring onion rounds, coriander and some sort of chilli condiment – the perfect foil to pumpkin's sweetness. The moru chilli sambol (page 37) or Lankan chilli crunch (page 39) would be my top picks. I've used a Japanese rice here, but you can substitute with your favourite grain, it may just change the texture slightly.

- 110 g (4 oz) sushi rice
- 45 g (1½ oz) ginger, ⅔ cut into a fine julienne, the rest left as a whole piece
- 8 g (¼ oz) salt flakes
- 700 g (1 lb 9 oz) piece Kent pumpkin (winter squash)
- 20 g (¾ oz) ghee
- 150 g (5½ oz) fresh grated coconut
- salt flakes and ground white pepper
- roti, cut into strips and fried, to serve
- spring onions (scallions), finely sliced, to serve
- coriander (cilantro), torn, to serve
- Moru chilli sambol (page 37) or Lankan chilli crunch (page 39), to serve

Wash and drain the rice, then place it in a medium heavy-based saucepan. Add the whole piece of ginger, the salt and 2 litres (68 fl oz) of water and bring to a boil before reducing to a gentle simmer. Cook for 40 minutes, stirring from time to time as it thickens.

Meanwhile, let's deal with the pumpkin. Preheat the oven to 180°C (360°F). Remove the seeds and cut the skin off. Grate a third of the pumpkin on the large holes of a box grater and set aside. Cut the remainder into medium-sized chunks, rub with ghee, season with salt and place on a baking tray. Cover with foil and bake until soft. Mash the pumpkin into a puree with a fork, then set aside.

Once the rice has been cooking for about 40 minutes, add the coconut and the grated pumpkin and give it a little stir. Cook for another 20 minutes, stirring occasionally, as the coconut can cause it to stick a little.

Add in the pureed pumpkin and the rest of the ginger, stir well and let the mixture heat back up.

At this stage it's just a matter of seasoning with pepper and more salt if needed and checking if the consistency is to your liking. This version is quite thick, but feel free to add more water if you desire.

Serve hot with accompaniments.

Corn kiribath with katta sambol

SERVES 6–8

Kiribath is a Lankan coconut milk rice served for celebrations and significant events. Or for breakfast. There's a whole thing you do on New Year's Eve that involves boiling the coconut milk so it overflows like your prosperity. There was a moment when corn was in season and Corentin was searching for ways to use it and he found versions of kiribath with corn in it, something I'd never seen. While he was testing it, Budi – our excellent Indonesian kitchen hand – suggested wrapping it in banana leaves to heat it before serving. And so here we have it.

- 4 ears of corn, cooked and kernels shucked
- 300 g (10½ oz) samba rice
- 1 star anise
- 3 cloves
- salt flakes
- 400 ml (13½ fl oz) coconut cream
- banana leaves, for wrapping
- Katta sambol (page 34), to serve

Gently pound the kernels in a mortar and pestle. Set aside.

Wash your rice and cook it according to your usual method, including the star anise, cloves and a little salt.

Once your rice is cooked, remove the whole spices, add the pounded corn and place this all in a medium saucepan along with the coconut cream and 350 ml (12 fl oz) of water.

Cook gently over a low–medium heat, stirring often, until the rice thickens and becomes sticky and there is no more liquid, about 20–25 minutes.

Turn the mixture out onto a tray, moulding it roughly into a 30–35 cm (12–13¾ in) square. Leave this to cool to room temperature and then place it in the fridge to set until firm.

Once set, cut the kiribath into 8 squares. Now at this stage I'm hoping you have some sort of hotplate or chargrill pan – a flat pan is ideal but a ridged one will also work. A barbecue is good, but the best would be a hibachi or some sort of coal or flame situation. If you have nothing like that, a large frying pan will work too. Whatever you are going to use, have it on a medium heat once your kiribath are ready to go.

Cut your banana leaves into an appropriate size, trimming the hard edge bit. You will need eight nice pieces around 26 x 28 cm (10¼ x 11 in) to wrap the kiribath. Heat the banana leaves slightly to make them pliable. At LFS we did this by placing them on a flat pan for a moment on each side – they changed colour and softened fairly quickly. At home, you can use an iron on a low setting to achieve the same result, or carefully wave them over a flame on your stovetop until they soften. Wrap each square of kiribath snugly so it is encased in banana leaf and set aside to come
to room temperature.

Place each square on the grill and sear it until the banana leaf starts to blacken and char, then flip over and repeat, the time will vary depending on what heat source you use. Slip the tip of a knife or a metal skewer into the middle to make sure the rice is nice and hot. If your banana leaves are looking too charred before the rice is ready, you can slip the parcels into the oven for a moment.

Serve it piping hot with katta sambol on the side, leaving your friends to peel open the leaf like an enticing present.

NOTE If you can't find samba rice, sushi rice is a good substitute.

Milk buns

MAKES 12–13

This handy little recipe is a good all-purpose one for making white, fluffy rolls. It's easy to do, and can be made in a few hours. They're super light when fresh, and freeze very well, although this does render their texture a little bit denser. The roll size below is quite small and perfect for the fried egg roll with fermented chilli sauce and pol sambol (page 84), but feel free to make slightly larger ones if you prefer – just note that you may need to cook them for a bit longer. You can also change the shape and size of the stuffed buns to suit your whim. The two recipes on pages 86–9 are merely a starting point for what you can stuff inside. Any curry would work well, as would the patty or pan roll fillings. Just make sure the stuffing isn't too wet, will hold its shape and has a bold flavour. Nobody wants a boring bun.

- 40 g (1½ oz) tepid water (no more than 27°C/80°F)
- 6 g (⅕ oz) dried active yeast
- 185 ml (6 fl oz) full-cream (whole) milk, plus 30 ml (1 fl oz) more
- 145 ml (5 fl oz) pouring (single/light) cream
- 470 g (1 lb 1 oz) plain (all-purpose) flour
- 40 g (1½ oz) caster (superfine) sugar
- 7 g (¼ oz) cooking salt
- 1 egg
- 80 g (2¾ oz) unsalted butter, melted

Place the water in a small mixing bowl and mix in the dried yeast to activate it.

Warm the milk and cream together in a small saucepan to 27°C (80°F). If you don't have a thermometer, it should be just warm enough that you can comfortably place your little finger in the liquid and leave it there for a moment.

Place the flour, sugar and salt in the bowl of a stand mixer fitted with a dough hook. On a slow speed, slowly pour in all the wet ingredients. Once fully combined, turn the mixer to medium and mix for 3–4 minutes, until the dough is smooth and comes away from the side of the bowl. You can also do this step by hand, though it may take a little longer.

Place the dough in a greased mixing bowl and leave it to proof in a slightly warm spot for 45 minutes, or until it has doubled in size.

Knock back the dough by giving it a few folds, then turn it out onto a clean bench. Use a pastry cutter or knife to cut the dough into 70 g (2½ oz) portions and roll each into a ball. (I would suggest having a little internet moment to see the best way to do this.)

Place the balls on a greased baking tray, then cover with a clean tea towel (dish towel) and allow to proof for about 15 minutes, until they bounce back when you gently poke them with your finger. By this stage they will be looking nice and plump.

Have your oven preheated to 180°C (360°F). Whisk together the egg and the remaining milk and gently brush over the tops of the buns. Bake for 15 minutes, turning the tray halfway through, then remove from the oven. Immediately brush the tops with melted butter, then brush twice more as the buns cool down. This gives both a nice gloss and some extra flavour to your buns.

The buns are ready once cooled.

NOTE Even though I have been cooking for a very long time I always thought there were just two types of the common yeast you use in baking: fresh or dried. It turns out, in Australia we have three: fresh yeast, instant dried yeast and active yeast (which confusingly is also dried ...) Fresh yeast has an appealing funky smell that I love but don't use very much as it's hard to come by. Active yeast, as the name implies, needs to be activated before it's used; this is why recipes ask you to soak the yeast in water, usually with sugar (which also helps to activate yeast) until it goes frothy. And then instant yeast is just that, ready to add straight in with no other faffing.

Fried egg roll with fermented chilli sauce and pol sambol

MAKES
2 PER PERSON

These little beauties are delicate in size (you'll probably need two per person), but not in eating – you will definitely get some egg on your face, and possibly your hands as well. The soft bun holds the egg, which is perfectly balanced in texture, crunchy on the outside and gooey in the middle. Pol sambol is a beautiful friend to the egg, and adding chilli sauce is highly encouraged. You can skip the bit where you make your own buns, but be sure to find the right substitute. They must be light and fluffy, and size is important here, as you need the right ratios; the bun should be about 70 g (2½ oz) in size, only just big enough to hold one egg.

- 2 buns per person
- 1 x quantity Curry leaf butter (page 57), for spreading
- 20 g (¾ oz) Pol sambol per bun (page 34)
- Fermented chilli sauce (page 62) and/or Pickled green chillies (page 53) for extra spice (optional)
- vegetable oil, for frying
- 2 eggs per person
- salt flakes

Split your buns in half and generously spread both sides with curry leaf butter. Spoon pol sambol onto the base. If you are using chilli sauce, spread this on the top half; if you are going to use pickled chillies, slice them into rounds ready to go.

Set yourself up with the wok method of frying eggs (see pages 73–5) and proceed, cooking the eggs one at a time. As they cook, place them onto a wire rack lined with paper towel and season with a sprinkle of salt flakes. Continue until you have enough eggs for everyone.

Working one bun at a time, carefully place an egg onto the base. Top with pickled chillies, if using, and pop the top on.

Eat with caution, as the yolk should be runny and messy.

Seeni sambol buns

MAKES 12–13

I first discovered a version of these on the breakfast buffet at a hotel, and they made me very happy. As you know, there is always too much food at a buffet, especially at breakfast, and not enough belly room, so I would eat my fill of hoppers and leave with several of the buns stashed in my pocket for morning tea. These are just one type of many filled buns you find in bakeries across the island, and they're my favourite, despite a pol sambol version I had recently (weirdly, in a hospital cafe), which was a strong contender.

- 1 x quantity Milk buns (page 82)
- 180 g (6½ oz) Seeni sambol (page 36)
- 1 egg
- 30 ml (1 fl oz) full-cream (whole) milk
- 60 g (2 oz) Curry leaf butter (page 57), melted

Follow the milk bun recipe until you get to the ball stage. Then ...

Place a dough ball on the bench and flatten it into a round about 5 mm (¼ in) thick. Place 15 g (½ oz) of the seeni sambol into the centre and use your fingers to pick up and pinch the dough over the filling, with the top meeting the bottom, then squeeze together the edges to form a small torpedo shape. Make sure the dough seam is nicely sealed.

Place the bun, seam side down, on a tray lined with baking paper. Repeat with the remaining dough and filling, making sure you leave enough room for spreading between the buns as they rise.

Let the buns proof again for another 10–15 minutes. To check, lightly press on the dough; if it springs back, they're ready.

Preheat the oven to 180°C (360°F). Whisk together the egg and milk and gently brush over the tops of the buns.

Bake for 15 minutes, turning the tray halfway through, then remove from the oven. Immediately brush the tops with melted curry leaf butter, then brush twice more as the buns cool down.

Seeni buns are delicious to eat while still warm, but can also be stored in the fridge or frozen. If doing this, gently heat them before eating.

Sausage buns

MAKES 42 X 70 G (2½ OZ) SAUSAGES OR 16 BUNS WITH SAUSAGES TO SPARE

This is really a recipe for a type of Lankan sausage, called lingus, laden with clove and textured with chunks of pork fat. These rich little stumpy beauties aren't for the pork-averse. This recipe will make many – I figure if you are going to the trouble of making your own sausages you may as well make plenty. Turn some or all of them into buns, or skip that bit entirely and serve them cut into pieces and skewered with toothpicks alongside a chilli sauce, like a Lankan bite. Alternatively, make them bigger and serve at a backyard barbecue. They freeze well and can be used like you would any other sausage. If you are going to turn them into buns, they are a bit like a baked hot dog; the ends of the sausage are strangely alluring, sticking out of the sides.

2 kg (4 lb 6 oz) coarse minced (ground) pork shoulder, cold

1 kg (2 lb 3 oz) pork back fat, cut into a 1 cm (½ in) dice, cold

30 g (1 oz) cooking salt

42 thick sausage casings

1 x quantity Milk bun dough (page 82)

1 egg

30 ml (1 fl oz) full-cream (whole) milk

60 g (2 oz) Curry leaf butter (page 57), melted

SPICE MIX

10 g (⅓ oz) black peppercorns

6 g (⅕ oz) cardamom seeds

4 g (⅛ oz) cloves

To make the spice mix, use a mortar and pestle to grind the spices until fine. Set aside.

Place the pork mince, back fat, salt and spice mix into a large bowl and combine. In batches, transfer to the bowl of a stand mixer fitted with the paddle attachment and start mixing slowly, then gradually increase the speed. Mix for 5 minutes until it has emulsified and looks like a sticky mass. (Keep the bowl with the rest of the mix in the fridge as you go.) Continue until all the mix is done.

Pipe the sausage mix into the sausage casings and tie off in about 10 cm (4 in) lengths (this should give you sausages that weigh about 70 g/2½ oz each), then hang them in your fridge to dry out overnight.

Once your sausages have hung out overnight, cut off sixteen ready to make into buns and rest them on paper towel nearby.

Follow the milk bun recipe to the stage just before cutting the dough ...

Cut the dough into 50 g (1¾ oz) portions and roll each portion into a sausage-like log about 10 cm (4 in) long.

Once all your dough is rolled, take a sausage and wrap a portion of the dough around it, overlapping and leaving a bit of sausage poking out of each end.

Place each bun on a tray lined with baking paper. Repeat with the remaining dough and sausages, making sure you leave a little room for spreading.

Let the buns proof again for another 10–15 minutes. To check, lightly press on the dough; if it springs back, they're ready.

Preheat the oven to 180°C (360°F). Whisk together the egg and milk and gently brush over the tops of the buns.

Bake for 15 minutes, turning the tray halfway through, then remove from the oven. Immediately brush the tops with melted curry leaf butter, then brush twice more as the buns cool down.

The buns are ready to eat as soon as they have cooled just a little, or not at all if you can't wait.

Jaffles, sandwiches and toasted roti

Any form of toasted bread, sandwich or roti wrap, when done properly, is usually delicious, and we should all give thanks to that card-playing earl from whence this all reportedly stems. In fact, the whole bread thing is so important we have devoted an entire chapter to it. The following recipes are for the ones you can hold in your hand, and are all things we served at LFS as brunch and lunch specials. Most of the filling combinations came about from using leftovers and stray things.

To start, we look at jaffles, that excellent Australian invention that is a toasted sandwich but one that must be made in a jaffle maker. The beauty of them lays in the fact that a jaffle maker seals the sides of the bread to cleverly encase the filling. This makes it perfect for adding sloppier options that would otherwise escape, the only hazard being that when you bite into it, the inside can ooze out at the temperature of molten lava. The hot tip when making a jaffle is that cheese is always good (particularly paired with a curry).

I've included a couple of sandwich ideas (can you really have a recipe for a sandwich?), both with many elements, and a little complicated if you are making them from scratch. They are made up of bits of recipes from this book, and they're delicious. Likewise, the toasted rotis here and from the restaurant are generally filled with things stolen from other parts of the menu.

The following recipes don't always give specific amounts, because the nature of sandwich making means that it often relies on leftovers. Besides, you could be making just one for yourself or a whole batch for a picnic. It's a bit of a choose your own adventure.

Jaffles

Mozzarella, cheddar and curry leaf

MAKES 1 SANDWICH

This was a toasted sandwich that debuted at Berta. I think it was an early step in my move to introduce more Lankan flavours into my 'Italian' menu, and it was so delicious that my Italian-leaning boss couldn't possibly complain. It is a simple and elegant jaffle that is equally happy as a toasted sandwich.

- Curry leaf butter (page 57), at room temperature
- 2 slices white bread
- ½ ball buffalo mozzarella, cut into slices
- 30 g (1 oz) grated cheddar
- salt flakes and freshly ground black pepper

Generously butter each slice of white bread on both sides and lay them on a board.

Cover one slice with mozzarella and sprinkle on the grated cheddar.

Season with a little salt and a heavy hand of pepper. Sandwich with the other slice of bread and cook in a jaffle maker until done.

Eat immediately.

Dhal and hot butter

MAKES 1 SANDWICH

This combination may sound a little strange, but it's surprisingly delicious. One of our easy kitchen breakfasts was a bowl of dhal with a spoon of hot butter drizzled over it to spice up the situation. Turning it into a jaffle seemed the obvious next step. Be warned though, the inside gets hotter than the surface of the sun, so take care on that first bite.

- 2 slices white bread
- Hot butter (page 57), at room temperature
- 120 g (4½ oz) cold Dhal (page 212)
- salt flakes and freshly ground black pepper

Butter each slice of bread on both sides. On one side, use just a sliver of the butter – this will be on the outside – but on the other side, go wild and use lashings.

Spoon the dhal onto the heavily buttered side of one slice, spreading it evenly.

Season with a little salt and a heavy hand of pepper. Sandwich with the other slice of bread and cook in a jaffle maker until done.

Eat immediately.

A FEW OTHER GOOD JAFFLE FILLING SUGGESTIONS

- Leftover crab (just the picked meat, obviously …) + lunu dehi
- Acharu + cheddar
- Any curry + cheddar
- Seeni sambol + mozzarella + cheddar
- Any of the patty fillings

Lankan bánh mì

MAKES – CHOOSE YOUR OWN ADVENTURE

A good bánh mì is a thing of beauty and easily one of my favourite sandwiches. One day, we had a Sri Lankan meatball curry on the menu at the same time as we'd made a batch of pâté. Before you knew it, here this was, our very own ode to bánh mì. I was very pleased. There are a lot of elements to this, and if you were making them all from scratch you would have a very long prep list. But this is a good dish if things collide, leaving you with the right combination of leftovers. As such, though, I haven't given specific amounts to anything – it's just a list of all the things that I would put into it and how to do.

- daikon (white radish)
- salt flakes
- caster (superfine) sugar
- cider vinegar
- salted butter
- Kade paan (page 106), or use a proper crunchy white roll that's soft in the middle
- Chicken liver pâté (page 118)
- Seeni sambol (page 36)
- meatballs from Meatball curry (page 178), at room temperature
- gotu kola (pennywort)
- fresh green chillies, cut into thin rounds
- spring onions (scallions), julienned
- coriander (cilantro) leaves, picked

Cut your daikon into thick matchsticks about ½ × 10 cm (¼ × 4 in). Place in a mixing bowl and season with salt flakes and a pinch of caster sugar – it should be gently salted. Mix through and let this sit for half an hour to soften. Squeeze the daikon and pour out any watery liquid, then season with a nice splash of cider vinegar. Set aside.

To construct your sandwich, first butter your bread or roll and then spread the base with a generous amount of pâté. Dollop seeni sambol onto the top piece of bread or roll and spread.

Place some meatballs on top of the pâté, followed by a layer of the daikon, then tear some gotu kola over the top. Add chillies to your liking and finish with a nice amount of spring onion and coriander, then top with the other slice of bread.

Eat immediately.

Reuben-ish

MAKES – CHOOSE YOUR OWN ADVENTURE

Unsurprisingly, this isn't really a Reuben sandwich, but if you look at each element you can see where the inspiration comes from. There's a roasted meat instead of a corned one, a cooked cabbage instead of a sauerkraut, and Edam cheese instead of Swiss. But please do use a nice light rye bread so we can at least pretend a little. This is another of those dishes that was easy to construct at the restaurant, as most of the elements were always there anyway; making everything from scratch could be daunting. And like the Lankan bánh mì (page 92) I don't give all the specific amounts; it's just a list of all the things that I would put into it and how to make it.

- salted butter
- a good light rye bread, lightly toasted
- Lunu dehi mayonnaise (page 35)
- Black spiced beef brisket (page 182), at room temperature or slightly warm
- Pickled green chillies (page 53), cut into rounds
- sliced Edam cheese

CABBAGE MALLUNG (ENOUGH FOR 3–4 SANDWICHES)

- 10 g (⅓ oz) ghee
- 5 g (⅕ oz) mustard seeds
- 2 g (1⁄16 oz) picked curry leaves
- 100 g (3½ oz) white cabbage, thinly sliced
- 1 g (1⁄32 oz) turmeric powder
- 20 g (¾ oz) grated coconut
- salt flakes and freshly ground black pepper

Make your cabbage mallung first, as you want this to be at room temperature when constructing your sandwich. Heat a wok or wide-based frying pan over a high heat, then add in the ghee, mustard seeds and curry leaves.

As soon as the mustard seeds start to pop and the curry leaves fry, add in the cabbage and give everything a good mix. Season heavily with salt and pepper.

After a few minutes, add the turmeric and continue stirring. Keep the cabbage moving over the high heat of the wok, but allow some moments of stillness to achieve a little char.

After another minute add the coconut, taste again for seasoning and cook for another 2–3 minutes, until the cabbage has wilted but still holds a little crunch. Set aside.

To construct your sandwich, generously butter two slices of bread and then spread both with a nice amount of the mayonnaise. Top one slice with a single layer of the brisket, then some mallung. Follow with the chillies to your liking, and season with a little salt and a good amount of black pepper. Top with the cheese and the other slice of bread.

Eat immediately.

Toasted godamba roti

I was very lucky to have found my perfect Sri Lankan grocery shop early on, way before I opened LFS. In Australia, good Lankan grocers can be hard to find without going to the outer edges of the suburbs, but this one is thankfully close to me. It's called Aum Spice, has been there for an age, and is run by a very lovely couple. They used to have a restaurant next door with Nira in the kitchen and Nathan on the floor. It has all the things I need, and Nathan is always ready to answer any silly question I may have. Nira still does some cooking for the shop. There is one crisp vadai she does which, despite explaining it to me, I have never been able to recreate anywhere near as good as she does. She also makes some of the best rotis I've had – they are a large, even, rectangular shape, beautifully flaky and have always been on the menu. If you want to do it like we do, you will have to go hunting for the perfect roti, or you could make your own (I know a good cookbook that has a recipe ...). The roti that we use and have based the following recipes on are 22 x 26 cm (8¾ × 10¼ in). See pictures opposite to clarify the filling, folding and cutting techniques that we use here.

Red onion, green chilli, saltbush and green tomato and cheddar

MAKES ENOUGH FOR 1 ROTI

This was one of the first toasted rotis we included on our brunch menu, and it still appears occasionally. The base is cooked off first, super savoury, hot with chilli and with a slightly bitter edge from the saltbush. The addition of cheddar brings it all together. When we first offered this, we gave people the option to add torn mozzarella, or bacon, diced and rendered down until crisp. Most sensible people would add both.

- 12 g (½ oz) ghee, plus extra for brushing
- 2 g (1⁄16 oz) picked curry leaves
- ½ medium red onion, thinly sliced
- 25 g (1½ oz) picked saltbush leaves
- ½–1 long green chilli, thinly sliced into rounds
- 1 small green tomato, cut in half and then into 3 mm (⅛ in) slices
- 1 roti (22 x 26 cm/8¾ × 10 ¼ in)
- 25 g (1 oz) cheddar, coarsely grated
- 30 g (1 oz) diced bacon, cooked until crisp (optional)
- ½ ball of mozzarella, torn (optional)
- salt flakes and freshly ground black pepper

Heat a large frying pan or wok over a high heat, then add in the ghee. Once the ghee is smoking, add the curry leaves, let them sizzle for a second and then add the onion, saltbush and chilli.

Cook, stirring often, and give it a season, making sure to use lots of black pepper. Continue cooking for 2–3 minutes, until the onions are softened and starting to caramelise, then add in the green tomato. Continue cooking for another 30 seconds, then remove from the heat and set aside.

Brush one side of your roti with ghee and place it, ghee-side down, on a hotplate or in a large frying pan over a medium heat. Spread the onion mix evenly along the middle third and then top with the cheddar. If you are using bacon or mozzarella, add these too.

By this stage the roti should be starting to brown. Use a large metal spatula to fold the roti into itself (see image, opposite), then flip the neat roti parcel to cook the other side.

The roti is ready once both sides are golden brown and crisp. Remove from the heat, cut into pieces and eat immediately.

Beetroot pickle, buffalo curd and cheddar

MAKES ENOUGH FOR 1 ROTI

I know I keep harping on about adding cheeses and pickles into toasted things, so here is an example of a particularly fine combination. The tricky thing is the buffalo curd. In Sri Lanka, the buffalo curd is a delicious yoghurt-like number, traditionally set in clay pots. This is not what I am speaking of here, though. At LFS we used a curd that is more like a set fresh cheese, vaguely similar in appearance to a smooth feta, which is mild with a delicate texture. That is what I mean here. If you can't find the curd, a feta would actually work, as would quark or haloumi.

- 1 roti (22 x 26 cm/8¾ × 10 ¼ in)
- ghee, for brushing
- 60 g (2 oz) buffalo curd
- 100 g (3½ oz) Beetroot pickle (page 52), drained
- 20 g (¾ oz) cheddar, grated
- salt flakes and freshly ground black pepper

Brush one side of your roti with ghee and place it, ghee-side down, on a hotplate or in a large frying pan over a medium heat.

Lay the buffalo curd in a single layer along the middle third of the roti, top with the beetroot and then the cheddar. Season with a little salt and lots of black pepper.

By this stage the roti should be starting to brown. Use a large metal spatula to fold the roti into itself, then flip the neat roti parcel to cook the other side.

The roti is ready once both sides are golden brown and crisp (see image, page 96). Remove from the heat, cut into pieces and eat immediately.

Greens, sprats and mozzarella

MAKES ENOUGH FOR 1 ROTI

This roti was inspired both by the classic Italian combination of bitter greens, anchovies and chillies, and a green vegetable dish that was staple on the menu, ours cooked with Maldive fish and whatever local greens were in season. If we were going for whimsical names, this would be called 'An Italian lost in Sri Lanka, hungry for lunch …'.

25 ml (¾ fl oz) olive oil
1 large garlic clove, roughly chopped
½–1 long red chilli, cut into thin rounds
60 g (2 oz) spigarello and chicory, washed and chopped (substitute with bitter greens of your liking)
20 g (¾ oz) sprats, fried until crisp
lime juice
1 roti (22 x 26 cm/8¾ × 10 ¼ in)
ghee, for brushing
½ ball of mozzarella, torn
salt flakes and freshly ground black pepper

Warm a frying pan over a medium heat, then add the olive oil and heat a little before adding in the garlic and chilli. Fry these off for a moment before adding in the greens. Season well. Turn the heat to high and cook the greens for about 3 minutes, until they char and wilt a little, before adding in the fried sprats. Combine well, give it a moment more to cook and then remove from the heat. Season with a good dash of lime juice and set aside.

Brush one side of your roti with ghee and place it, ghee-side down, on a hotplate or in a large frying pan over a medium heat.

Spread the green mix evenly along the middle third of the roti, top with the mozzarella and season well.

By this stage the roti should be starting to brown. Use a large metal spatula to fold the roti into itself (see image, page 96), then flip the neat roti parcel to cook the other side.

The roti is ready once both sides are golden brown and crisp. Remove from the heat, cut into pieces and eat immediately.

Black spiced brisket, iceberg, acharu and lunu dehi mayonnaise

MAKES ENOUGH FOR 1 ROTI

This roti wrap came into being when I was doing some recipe testing before LFS opened. I had just cooked a black spiced meat curry, one of my favourites, which has been a staple on the menu since we opened, and it was sitting in the fridge next to a packet of roti. It was lunchtime and I was hungry, and so, with a little sliced iceberg and some mayonnaise, this was born. *Oh,* I thought to myself, *I must remember this one* – and so I did. It eventually appeared on the menu in fairly regular rotation with a few extra bits to make it a little more fancy. The black spiced beef brisket works here just as well as the black spiced curry we usually use.

1 roti (22 x 26 cm/8¾ × 10 ¼ in)
ghee, for brushing
Black spiced beef brisket (page 182), cut into slices, at room temperature (about 190 g/6½ oz worth)
Lunu dehi mayonnaise (page 35)
50 g (1¾ oz) Karkalla acharu (page 52)
100 g (3½ oz) iceberg lettuce, finely shredded
fermented chilli sauce (optional)
salt flakes and freshly ground black pepper

Brush one side of your roti with ghee and place it, ghee side down, on a hotplate or in a large frying pan over a medium heat.

Lay your brisket slices out along the short side. Let it sit to warm the brisket and allow the roti to start crisping along the bottom, then carefully remove the roti from the heat and lay it on a board.

Spread the mayonnaise along the exposed surface of the roti, almost to the edge. Top the brisket with the karkalla, then the iceberg and some chilli sauce, if you desire. Season well.

Working from the brisket edge, tightly roll it all together to form a wrap. Eat immediately.

AT

ANY

TIME

THINGS ON, NEXT TO AND IN BETWEEN KADE PAAN

I would just like to apologise to our gluten-free friends, who may need to look away from this chapter where we celebrate a very particular Sri Lankan bread. (Although fear not, you could make most of these recipes and serve them with a nice leaf, or even a piece of gluten-free bread if you so desire, or just get the vibe of the flavours and adapt.) Kade paan, shop bread, is the simple, ubiquitous, much-eaten loaf of Sri Lanka. It is a soft, fluffy white number, made with butter and traditionally roasted in a woodfired oven. Some versions are super white, soft, light and fluffy, so much so that a large slice can be squashed to nothing. Others have a bit more heft to them, but only slightly so. You can buy kade paan fresh daily from bakeries and shops, or more excitingly from the back of customised tuk-tuks that roam the streets. They are laden with bakery goods, proudly packed into the glass display cabinets built onto their backs, and blare Beethoven's 'Für Elise' in their wake.

The whole bread thing arrived in Sri Lanka courtesy of the Portuguese in the sixteenth century, the word 'paan' derived from the Portuguese 'pao'. Now it is everywhere. It becomes a stand-in for rice eaten at any meal with foods as simple as a pol sambol or a dhal, or as an accompaniment to curries.

As much as I love a good chewy sourdough and the health of heavy grains, I do still feel there is a time and a place for a good piece of white fluff.

'At any time' means exactly that. These dishes are good slipped in anywhere. Some I'd eat for breakfast, others brunch, some for pre-dinner, others even as an easy snack-like dinner on their own. Sometimes there are no rules. The following recipes can be subbed in with white fluffy bread of your choice. This is a moment when supermarket bread comes into its own – use the thick-sliced one.

NOTE The kade paan is quite a large loaf so if you are subbing in other bread, the amounts may vary.

Kade paan

MAKES 1 LOAF

Here it is, the white fluffy bread of your dreams. It's a handsome loaf.

- **10 g (⅓ oz) dried active yeast**
- **30 g (1 oz) caster (superfine) sugar**
- **80 ml (2½ fl oz) lukewarm water, to mix the yeast**
- **595 g (1 lb 5 oz) plain (all-purpose) flour**
- **12 g (½ oz) cooking salt**
- **410 ml (14 fl oz) lukewarm water for the dough**
- **40 g (1½ oz) unsalted butter, diced, at room temperature**

FOR THE TOP

- **80 g (2¾ oz) butter, melted**
- **30 g (1 oz) plain (all-purpose) flour**
- **20 ml (¾ fl oz) olive oil**

You will need a large loaf tin for this recipe; I use one that is 27 x 13.5 cm (10¾ x 5¼ in) with a depth of 10 cm (4 in). This makes a loaf with a height of about 12.5 cm (5 in). Oil your tin and set aside.

Mix the yeast and sugar with the tepid water and let it bloom for around 5–10 minutes, until frothy.

Place the flour, salt, water and the yeast mixture in a stand mixer fitted with a dough hook. Mix on a slow speed until the mix just forms a sticky dough, then add in the softened butter a little at a time as you continue to mix for roughly 30 minutes. The dough will start coming away from the sides of the bowl at about the halfway mark, but you need to continue until the sides of the bowl look completely clean, at which stage the dough will be nice and elastic.

When all the butter is mixed in, turn the mixer up to low–medium and mix for roughly 10 minutes, until the dough is nice and elastic and pulls away from the side of the bowl. Try not to let the dough get too hot.

Cover the dough and let it rise for 45 minutes at a warm room temperature (21–24°C/70–75°F is perfect). It should double in size.

Oil your hands and turn the dough out onto your bench. It will be quite sticky but knock it back, fold it into a ball and rest it on the bench for another 15 minutes or so.

Pat out the dough into a rectangle. You want the top edge to be the length of the tin and the sides stretched down until the dough is about 3 cm (1¼ in) in height. Roll this into a tight cylinder and place it seam-side down into your bread tin.

Cover loosely and let the dough proof for another 45 minutes to 1 hour, at which stage it should have reached the top of the tin and will look light, fluffy and a bit bubbly. Poke it gently with your finger and it should bounce back slightly, but if your fingertip remains defined it is probably over-proofed a bit. It will still work, but it won't rise as much when cooking and will be a little more dense.

Preheat the oven to 200°C (390°F), and pop a tray in the bottom of the oven while it is heating up.

Whisk the butter, flour and oil for the top together and then generously brush this onto the exposed top of the dough.

To bake, place the bread tin in the oven and throw a few cubes of ice onto the tray you have been warming. This will create some steam, which will help at the start of the bake. Bake the bread for 30–40 minutes, until crusty and brown. (A probe thermometer inserted into the centre of the bread should read 90°C/195°F.) Turn the tin halfway through to ensure even baking.

Remove from the oven and turn out onto a wire cake rack to cool before slicing.

Asparagus and mustard rolls

MAKES 16 ROLLS

I first heard of these when my mum started describing the canapes my nan used to serve at her glamorous cocktail parties in Colombo in the 1960s and 70s. I thought it was a Lankan thing, but when I made them at LFS there was a general murmuring of approval among many customers of a certain age from other parts of the world. I believe canned asparagus was the rage back then, but we can do better than that. Make this at the height of asparagus season, when the stalks are nice and juicy.

- 16 asparagus spears, medium-sized
- olive oil
- 8 slices fresh Kade paan (page 106), cut into 1.5 cm (½ in) slices
- salt flakes and freshly ground black pepper

MUSTARD BUTTER

- 120 g (4½ oz) salted butter, softened
- 40 g (1½ oz) Mustard (page 44)
- 60 g (2 oz) cheddar, grated finely

First make your mustard butter by combining the butter, mustard and cheddar in a mixing bowl until smooth. Set aside.

Blanch your asparagus spears in a large saucepan of gently boiling salted water until they are cooked through and on the softer side of just done, about 2–3 minutes. Transfer to a bowl of iced water until cold, then lay them out on some paper towel and pat them dry. Transfer the spears to a tray, drizzle with just a splash of olive oil and season well. Roll the spears around to cover them – they shouldn't be swimming in oil, they just need a slight gloss.

To construct, lay out your kade paan and spread each slice generously with the mustard butter (making sure you use it all; I know it's a lot but it's necessary). Cut off the crusts and snack on them as you go.

Lay two spears of asparagus along the bottom of each slice with a head on either side. The spears will be longer than the bread and should poke out a little at each end. Tightly roll your slice of bread around the asparagus, gently pressing down on the edge of the bread to seal it. Lay out your rolls seam-side down as you complete each one.

Once constructed, cut each roll evenly into half and serve them on their sides, sitting up like a little forest of asparagus trees.

Curried egg sandwiches

MAKES 4 SANDWICHES

As a child, Chazzy, my Mum, and I went on many long car trips. At the time I felt tortured by having to visit each and every sight along the way when I would have much preferred to be left to sleep or to continue reading, as I was wont to do. But it was obligatory, as were the curried egg sandwiches she would insist upon bringing, which I refused to eat. Travel for hours in an un-air-conditioned car in an Australian summer, and smell what that does to an egg sandwich and you will understand. Now though, I am quite partial to both an egg sandwich and a scenic sight.

- 6 eggs
- 3 g (1⁄10 oz) picked curry leaves, fried
- 100 g (3½ oz) eschalots, finely diced
- 3 small green chillies, finely sliced
- 20 g (¾ oz) White curry powder (page 26)
- 20 g (¾ oz) Mustard (page 44)
- 70 g (2½ oz) mayonnaise
- salt flakes and ground white pepper
- 1 x quantity Fermented chilli powder (page 63) (optional)
- 8 slices of fresh Kade paan (page 106), cut into 1.8 cm (½ in) slices
- salted butter, softened, for spreading

Cook the eggs in a pot of boiling water for 8 minutes, then transfer to a bowl of iced water to cool.

Peel the eggs, place them in a mixing bowl and use a fork to coarsely mash them.

Add in the curry leaves, eschalots, chillies, curry powder, mustard and mayonnaise and thoroughly mix. Season well adding some fermented chilli powder, if you happen to have some.

Spread your bread generously with butter, then divide the egg mixture evenly over four slices, making sure to spread it right to the edge. Top each slice with a lid. Cut off the crusts (for you to snack on), and then cut your sandwiches into halves, fingers or triangles, whatever suits you best. These are best eaten super fresh, so they don't get hot and stinky in the sun.

Cheese toast

MAKES
4 SLICES

This was a late addition to the book, but thankfully made it just in the nick of time. I was lucky enough to be in Sri Lanka while in the midst of writing, and somebody ordered this for me at The Colombo Swimming Club. It was very delicious and made me happy, but it also made me wonder why no one had ever told me about this delightful dish before. Basically, it's a version of cheese on toast, but Lankified. I've read various recipes, which may contain butter or not, cream, an egg, but always chilli, onion and sometimes capsicum. Anyhow, as I was extolling the virtues of this dish and busy being upset about the years I've gone without it, a good friend told me I was being ridiculous, as he'd made me eat it before. He then proceeded to tell me of all the clubs I needed to visit in order to sample other versions. Sadly I had run out of time, leaving me with just the one lingering taste to call upon when making my own version.

- 100 g (3½ oz) cheddar, grated on the large holes of a box grater
- 50 g (1¾ oz) parmesan, finely grated
- 100 ml (3½ fl oz) pouring (single/light) cream
- 2 eggs
- 80 g (2¾ oz) eschalots, finely diced
- 2 green bird's eye chillies, finely chopped
- salt flakes and freshly ground black pepper
- 4 slices Kade paan (page 106), cut into 2 cm (¾ in) thick pieces
- Curry leaf butter (page 57), softened, for spreading

Place all ingredients except the bread and curry leaf butter in a small mixing bowl and thoroughly combine. Season well.

Under a grill, toast both sides of your bread just a little (or use a toaster). Remove from the grill and preheat the oven to 200°C (390°F).

Butter your slices of bread well and then top with the cheese mixture. Place them onto a baking tray and pop them into the oven to cook for 10 minutes, until the mix is golden brown and oozy. Give them an extra moment under a hot grill for extra colour, if you desire.

Slice into thirds and eat immediately.

Crab toasts

MAKES 12 FINGERS

I have done many variations of crab and toast, from when I was being Italian at Berta, where I called it bruschetta, to my favourite jaffle at LFS, made with leftover crab curry and lunu dehi. Eating picked crab is such a luxury, the delicate flesh divested of the shell is a real treat. Your options for crab here are to pick any leftovers you may have from the mud crab you cooked (see page 161), buy it picked, or buy a raw crab and pick it yourself. Obviously, the last option is both the most time-consuming and the best. This combination is a good one, though, a tart, sharp mayonnaise, a slightly sweet pickle and some gotu kola, adding some tough bitterness to give it a bit of an edge. It's a good fancy pre-dinner snack that would go very nicely with a glass or two of champagne to celebrate life.

- 300 g (10½ oz) raw picked crabmeat or 260 g (9 oz) cooked picked crabmeat
- 60 g (2 oz) Jackfruit acharu (page 50), cut into strips
- 10 g (⅓ oz) gotu kola, very thinly shredded
- salt flakes and ground white pepper
- 4 slices Kade paan (page 106), cut into 2 cm (¾ in) slices
- Lunu dehi mayonnaise (page 35), for spreading
- fried curry leaves, to garnish

If you are cooking the crabmeat, preheat the oven to 150°C (300°F). Spread the crabmeat onto a tray lined with baking paper, drizzle with a little olive oil and cook for about 3–4 minutes, until it's just cooked.

Place the crabmeat into a small mixing bowl with the jackfruit and gotu kola, season and gently mix.

Toast your bread until it is medium brown, then let it cool slightly over a wire rack. Generously spread each slice with the lunu dehi mayonnaise, then top with the crab mix and garnish with the fried leaves.

Slice each piece of bread into three fingers and serve immediately.

Prawn toast with sweet chilli sauce

MAKES 8 CHUNKY HALVES

Prawn toast is one of those dishes that's a people pleaser. Everyone loves a prawn, and being deep-fried and on bread makes this an easy sell. It feels like a guilty pleasure. When you look at the usual ingredients a prawn toast is made with, it is very easy to see how it only takes a little bending to push it towards Sri Lankan flavours. Just add curry powder and curry leaves ...

- 500 g (1 lb 2 oz) peeled prawn (shrimp) meat, finely chopped
- 50 g (1¾ oz) eschalots, finely diced
- 50 g (1¾ oz) spring onions (scallions), cut into thin rounds
- 20 g (¾ oz) peeled ginger, julienned
- 5 g (⅕ oz) picked curry leaves, julienned
- 4 small green chillies, finely chopped
- 14 g (½ oz) fine rice flour
- 10 g (⅓ oz) sesame oil
- 10 g (⅓ oz) caster (superfine) sugar
- 5 g (⅕ oz) White curry powder (page 26)
- 1 bunch coriander (cilantro), root and stems washed and finely chopped, leaves picked
- salt flakes and ground white pepper
- 4 slices Kade paan (page 106), cut into 1.8 cm (½ in) slices
- Curry leaf butter (page 57), softened, for spreading
- vegetable oil, for frying

SWEET CHILLI SAUCE

- 100 g (3½ oz) caster (superfine) sugar
- 3 large, dried chillies, split in half
- 40 ml (1¼ fl oz) coconut vinegar
- 3–5 bird's eye chillies, finely sliced

To make the chilli sauce, place the caster sugar in a small saucepan with 75 ml (2½ fl oz) of water and bring to a boil. Add the dried chillies and let the mix simmer for 30 minutes, until it thickens. Allow it to cool completely, then add the coconut vinegar to season. You want it to have a sour-sweet balance, with the syrup still a little thick. Place the syrup into a nice serving ramekin, fishing out the dried chillies and adding in the bird's eye chillies. Set aside until you are ready to serve.

Place the prawn meat in a bowl along with all the other ingredients up to the coriander (add the stem and root here, and reserve the leaves) and mix well. Season to taste, being heavy handed with the white pepper.

Spread each slice of bread generously with curry leaf butter and then top with the prawn mix. You want a thick, even layer.

Fill a wide and shallow saucepan up to 4 cm (1½ in) with oil and heat to 170°C (340°F). Fry the toasts in batches, turning halfway to cook evenly, for about 4–5 minutes, until the toast is golden and the prawn mix is cooked. Transfer to a wire rack, prawn-side up.

Cut each slice into half and serve immediately with coriander leaves unnecessarily strewn over the top and some of the sauce on the side.

Chicken liver pâté with arrack and black pepper

MAKES – A LARGE AMOUNT OF PÂTÉ

I have been cooking a version of this pâté since I first encountered it very early on in my career. It is silky and rich and not like anything in Sri Lanka at all. I really love it though, so I tweaked the ingredients just enough to be able to justify putting it on the menu at LFS. The clincher was when we discovered just how well it went with seeni sambol. After that, I felt completely at ease. This recipe makes one large log, or you can also cook the mix in small jars or moulds, producing smaller portions that you can give to your friends.

- 60 g (2 oz) ghee
- 7 g (¼ oz) picked curry leaves
- 200 g (7 oz) eschalots, sliced
- 40 g (1½ oz) finely chopped garlic
- 3 fresh bay leaves
- 400 ml (13½ fl oz) arrack
- 1 kg (2 lb 3 oz) cleaned chicken livers
- 100 ml (3½ fl oz) coconut cream
- 2 eggs
- 400 g (14 oz) unsalted butter, melted and cooled slightly
- 20 g (¾ oz) salt flakes
- 1.5 g (1⁄20 oz) sodium nitrate

SPICE MIX

- 5 g (⅕ oz) black peppercorns
- 2 g (1⁄16 oz) cinnamon
- 1 g (1⁄32 oz) cloves

TO SERVE

- Seeni sambol (page 36)
- Pickled cherries (page 53)
- Kade paan, toasted (page 106)
- olive oil, to drizzle, and freshly ground black pepper

NOTE The sodium nitrate is in this recipe as it helps the pâté keep its glorious pink colour. It can be happily omitted but your pâté will oxidise faster; however, this only affects the look not the taste. Another way to stop the edges of your pâté oxidising is to line your mould with thinly sliced pork back fat, or if you are making it in small jars, by pouring a little ghee or clarified butter on the top to seal it.

To make your spice mix, finely grind the spices together in a mortar and pestle, and set aside.

Warm a small frying pan over a low heat, and then add the ghee. Once the ghee is hot, add in the curry leaves and let them fry for a moment, then add the eschalot, garlic, bay leaves and spice mix. Cook, stirring often, until the eschalot has softened – you don't want any colour.

Add in the arrack and continue cooking for about 5 minutes, until it's mostly evaporated. The mixture should still look moist but not wet.

Remove from the heat, pick out the bay leaves and allow to cool completely.

Once cool, place the eschalot mixture into a Thermomix or blender along with the livers. Blend until super smooth and then, in quick succession while the blender is still running, add the coconut cream and then the eggs. Quickly follow with the warmed, melted butter, pouring it in a steady stream, and then finish with the salt and sodium nitrate. As soon as everything is incorporated, turn the blender off.

Pour the mix into a drum sieve and use a rubber spatula or pastry card to push it through.

Preheat the oven to 110°C (230°F).

Line a terrine mould or a small loaf tin 8 x 33 x 7 cm (3¼ × 13 × 2¾ in) with plastic wrap, using oil to make it stick. Make sure you have some overhang on each edge. Pour in the pâté mix, and then gently fold over the overhang to cover. Tightly cover the top of the mould with foil.

Place your pâté into a large tray filled with enough hot water to come about halfway up the sides of your pâté mould. This will ensure the pâté cooks gently. Cook in the oven for 40–60 minutes, until the internal temperature reaches 59–61°C (136–144°F). The time it takes will vary wildly depending on your oven, how hot the liver mix is when you pour it in and the shape and size of your pâté mould (especially if you are making multiple small ones).

Once cooked, remove the mould or tin from the water, remove the foil and let the pâté cool to room temperature before placing it in the fridge to fully cool.

Remove the pâté from the fridge and carefully remove it from the mould by jiggling it out using the plastic. The pâté is now ready to be sliced. It will last for a good three weeks if kept well wrapped in the fridge.

Serve a slice with a mound of seeni sambol, some pickled cherries and toasted kade paan. Give everything a little drizzle of olive oil and an extra sprinkle of ground black pepper.

The buffalo herder

This isn't so much a recipe with amounts, more a gathering of ingredients. It is based on the idea of a ploughman's lunch, which I love, particularly for breakfast. The whole idea of having numerous savoury elements that you are free to mix and match at whim seems very sensible to me. A bit of cured meat, some cheese and pickles, and add a boiled egg if you desire. Or serve it for dinner and call it Sri Lankan antipasti.

- mortadella, thinly sliced
- Pickled mustard seeds (page 54)
- a strong bitey cheddar, cut into thick slices
- fresh radishes, whole or cut into chunks, keep the leaves attached if they are worthy
- Pineapple chutney (page 55)
- Karkalla acharu (page 52)
- Kade paan (page 106), cut into 1.5 cm (½ in) slices, toasted with a bit of char
- olive oil
- salt flakes

This is really a gathering, so you are free to arrange at your whim. My only request is once you arrange the mortadella, spoon the pickled mustard seeds over the top with a little of their juice. Also, finish the whole plate with a good drizzle of olive oil and a sprinkle of salt.

SHORT EATS AND BITES

DOUSE ME IN CHILLI AND CALL ME DEVILLED

Are snacks not one of the greatest pleasures of life? Little morsels of flavour designed to easily pop in the mouth. Small and bite-sized, allowing you to graze without getting the food fatigue that can come with a large plate of the same thing. Sri Lankans have cleverly got two expressions for these: short eats, which you can pop into your mouth with one hand while you're on the go, and bites, which are a bit more substantial – a small plate of something, there to be shared but eaten with a fork in hand, leaving the other free to hold a drink.

One of the thrills about dishes in this realm is that they are inherently naughty. You aren't looking for anything as practical as a balanced nutritional meal; here, it's all about strong bursts of flavour, hot and spicy and usually a little bit salty, whetting the appetite rather than filling you up.

That's what makes this section so fun – it offers all sorts of easy ways to play with Sri Lankan flavours. One of the great food terms on the island is the naming of a dish 'devilled ...'. Insert nearly any ingredient here, from cashews to chicken – you name it, it's been devilled. It's a lovely term that covers almost anything and simply means something that is cooked with chilli, and usually a dry-fried dish. So you can see how this leaves endless room for interpretation. We have a pan roll and some patties here, their shape and appearance giving them their name. What goes in is entirely up to us, again leaving an excellent opening to play with non-traditional ingredients. Some of the recipes are inspired from elsewhere. What they all have in common, though, is strong spicy flavours that will make your mouth sing.

Devilled olives

SERVES 6–8

I'm not sure why, but I always find it confusing that they have olives in Sri Lanka. It seems incongruous somehow. But although they look similar to the olives we know and love, they are a fruit indigenous to the island and a slightly different beast. The texture is a bit grainy, the flavour slightly sour, and they're usually turned into an acharu. I have never been able to get the fruit here, but I am particularly partial to an olive, so I worked with what we could get and created this. Find your favourite firm, large green brined olive for this recipe.

- 320 g/11½ oz (drained weight) green kalamata or bella di cergola olives
- 40 ml (1¼ fl oz) olive oil
- 3 g (1⁄10 oz) chilli powder
- 3 g (1⁄10 oz) chilli flakes
- freshly ground black pepper

Drain your olives, and if they are on the salty side give them a quick wash in cold water. Use the flat side of a knife to gently crush each olive slightly, making sure the flesh of the olive still holds to the seed.

Place them in a mixing bowl, pour over the olive oil, give the olives a mix, sprinkling in the chilli powder and flakes.

Preheat the oven to 120°C (250°F). Lay the olives onto a baking tray and season well with black pepper. Let them gently cook for 1½ hours. By this stage they will have dried out a little and sucked in all that chilli flavour.

Remove from the oven and allow to cool slightly before serving. These olives can be served warm, at room temperature or cold – any way is good.

Devilled macadamias

SERVES 6–8

Devilled nuts are an extremely common street snack, and rightly so. A warm salty nut, particularly one laced with chilli, is the perfect drinking snack, no? In Sri Lanka, it's their glorious plump fresh cashews that so often get this treatment. In Australia, the native macadamia reigns supreme, and its buttery richness with a hint of sweetness works perfectly with this salty, chilli-laden treatment.

- 400 g (14 oz) whole raw macadamias
- 40 g (1½ oz) ghee
- 12 g (½ oz) mustard seeds
- 6 g (1⁄5 oz) picked curry leaves
- 8 g (¼ oz) salt flakes
- 5 g (1⁄5 oz) chilli flakes
- 6 g (1⁄5 oz) chilli powder

Preheat the oven to 160°C (320°F). Roast the macadamias on a lined baking tray for around 15–20 minutes, giving them a jiggle every 5 minutes to ensure even cooking, until they reach an even pale brown colour.

Set aside to cool. (Note, this step can be done in advance.)

Heat a large frying pan over a medium heat. Add the ghee and mustard seeds and cook, jiggling your pan, until the mustard seeds just start to pop.

Add in the curry leaves and let them fry a little, stirring for a minute before adding in the cooled macadamias.

Give the nuts a good stir to coat them in the ghee, then add in the salt.

Fry the macadamias for just a moment before adding in the chilli flakes and continue cooking and stirring for 30 seconds.

Remove from the heat and stir through the chilli powder.

Allow to cool just enough to easily eat with your fingers, or store in an airtight container to eat later. If you do choose to store them, make sure to mix well before serving.

Sprats and peanuts

SERVES 6–8

Ikan bilis is a very excellent Malaysian garnish or snack. It's one of those perfect combinations – crunchy, salty and a little bit sticky. It is just as delicious to eat by the fingerful as it is with a simple bowl of rice, needing almost nothing else to make a simple meal. As my restaurant was so often a conduit for my food cravings, I decided a Lankan version of this was needed.

- vegetable oil, for deep-frying
- 250 g (9 oz) sprats
- 250 g (9 oz) small whole raw peanuts, skin on
- 10 g (¼ oz) moru chillies
- 110 g (4 oz) peeled brown onion, roughly chopped
- 20 g (¾ oz) long red chilli, roughly cut
- 10 g (¼ oz) peeled garlic
- 20 g (¾ oz) ghee
- 14 g (½ oz) picked curry leaves
- 25 g (1 oz) jaggery, finely chopped or grated
- 7 g (¼ oz) tamarind concentrate or paste
- 4 g (⅛ oz) chilli powder
- salt flakes and freshly ground black pepper

Heat the oil in a wide-based saucepan to 160°C (320°F) and fry your sprats, in batches if necessary, for about 2–3 minutes, until crisp. Transfer to a wire cake rack lined with paper towel to drain.

Repeat with the peanuts, which will take about 2–3 minutes, then drain them on the rack with the sprats.

Next, fry the moru chillies in the same oil – these will take about 1–2 minutes. Drain these separately on some paper towel, then cut them roughly into small slices. Set aside.

In a Thermomix or blender, blend the onion, red chilli and garlic until the mixture forms a paste. Transfer the paste to a fine strainer and leave it to drain for at least 30 minutes.

Once all these elements are ready to go, you can start the final cooking.

Warm a large, wide-based saucepan over a medium heat, then add in the ghee. Once the ghee is shimmering, add the curry leaves and let them fry for about 30 seconds, stirring as you go. Add in the strained onion paste and continue cooking, stirring constantly, for about 5 minutes, until the mixture becomes aromatic.

Add in the jaggery and continue stirring for about 5 minutes, until the mixture starts to caramelise and stick. Add the tamarind and chilli powder, mix, and then add in the fried sprats, peanuts and moru chillies. Reduce the heat to low and give the mixture a thorough yet gentle stir, making sure everything is well mixed and coated. Add salt and pepper to season. Remove from the heat.

Once the mix has cooled, it's ready to eat. It will last for several months stored in an airtight container.

Caramelised kithul and fermented chilli popcorn

SERVES 6–8

One of my favourite treats as a small person was lolly gobble bliss bombs. Remember those? A silver packet with sweet, toffeed popcorn. Well, this is almost like a grown-up version of that, the sweetness tempered with a subtle chilli and salty kick, making it more of a grown-up snack for drinks. Or just a good snack to have at any time.

- 40 g (1½ oz) ghee
- 100 g (3½ oz) popping corn kernels
- 200 ml (7 fl oz) kithul
- 10 g (⅓ oz) Fermented chilli powder (page 63)
- salt flakes and freshly ground black pepper
- 10 g (⅓ oz) picked curry leaves, fried

Pop your corn using the ghee. You may have your own method, but my hot tip is to have the saucepan on a medium heat with the ghee, in along with three kernels of corn. Once the first kernel pops, add in the rest of the corn and give it a stir. Place the lid on the saucepan and reduce the heat to low. Cook until all the kernels are popped.

Once the corn is popped, place it in a large mixing bowl.

Meanwhile, place the kithul in a small saucepan along with the fermented chilli powder and simmer until the mixture is thick and sticky and reduced by half.

Preheat the oven to 100°C (210°F). Pour the reduced kithul over the popped corn, season with salt and pepper and mix well. Once you are happy with the flavour, fold through the curry leaves, then transfer the popcorn to a tray lined with baking paper. Place in the oven and leave it to dry out and sit for 1 hour.

Serve warm.

Oysters with lime pickle mignonette

MAKES ENOUGH SAUCE FOR 1–2 DOZEN OYSTERS

Sri Lanka has its own oysters, but for some reason I have never eaten any there and I have no idea why. But in Sydney, with our small and delicately flavourful Sydney Rocks, you can't stop me. Starting a meal or a banquet with an oyster or even just a plate of oysters with a drink is a clever way to go. To my mind, a freshly shucked oyster needs little else; however, a mignonette sauce is a very happy friend. My version is not far off the original, we've just spiked it with a little lime pickle, giving an extra salty and sharp kick, which is a lovely seamless match with a briny oyster.

- 1 pickled lime
- approximately 30 g (1 oz) eschalots, finely diced
- ground white pepper
- 50 ml (1¾ fl oz) cider vinegar
- juice of 1 lime
- 12–24 freshly shucked oysters, cold

Cut out the pulp from your pickled lime and set it aside to use for something else. Finely dice the skin and place it in a mixing bowl.

Add the eschalot, adjusting the quantity if needed – you are aiming to have equal parts lime to onion. Add lots of pepper and the vinegar and mix to combine. Finish with a little lime juice, to taste.

To serve, lay the oysters out on a platter with the dressing to the side so people can add as desired.

Crab varai on betel leaf

MAKES 20 BETEL LEAVES

Every time I go to Sri Lanka, I seem to discover at least one new dish that sticks with me. One time it was a prawn varai dish at an old-school Jaffna restaurant in Colombo. It was under the sambol section, the dish a jumble of fresh coconut and cooked prawn pieces seasoned with mustard seeds, turmeric, dried chilli and lime. It was fresh, light and super delicious. As soon as I got back to LFS I put a version on our menu, using crab instead, and turning it into a short eat by serving a mound of it on a betel leaf, adding a delightful bitter edge to the bite. Be warned though, if you try to recreate this dish while in Sri Lanka, what we call betel leaves are not the same as what they call them (bite into one at a market stall like I did and you will quickly realise why they are only for chewing) – find what they call a pepper leaf instead. For this recipe I would suggest using raw crabmeat and cooking it yourself, to ensure it's only just cooked. If that's too tricky though, use pre-cooked. Either way, people are going to be impressed.

- 20 medium-sized betel leaves
- 30 ml (1 fl oz) grapeseed oil
- 3 g (1/10 oz) mustard seeds
- 50 g (1¾ oz) eschalots, finely diced
- 15 g (½ oz) garlic, finely chopped
- 3½ long dried chillies, finely sliced
- 3 g (1/10 oz) picked curry leaves, finely sliced
- 170 g (6 oz) fresh grated coconut
- 2 g (1/16 oz) turmeric powder
- salt flakes and freshly ground black pepper
- 180 g (6½ oz) picked crabmeat
- 1–2 limes

To start, have your betel leaves washed, dried and ready to go.

Place a medium frying pan over a gentle heat and add in the oil. Once warmed, add in the mustard seeds and fry off for about 30 seconds, until they're popping. Add in the eschalot, garlic, chilli and curry leaves and stir, then add the coconut, turmeric and seasoning. Cook off this base for about 2 minutes, then remove from the heat and transfer to a small mixing bowl.

If you are cooking the crabmeat yourself, preheat the oven to 150°C (300°F). Spread the crabmeat out on a tray in an even layer and drizzle with a little olive oil and seasoning. Cook in the oven for about 2 minutes – you want it to be only just cooked. Add the crabmeat to the coconut mix. If you are using pre-cooked crabmeat, make sure it's at room temperature before you add it.

Season with a squeeze of lime juice and mix well, then taste. You want to make sure there's a nice amount of black pepper and a zing of fresh lime in there.

Place a generous spoonful of the mixture onto the centre of each betel leaf, making sure to divide the filling evenly.

Eat immediately, picking up the leaves, wrapping them around the filling and popping into your mouth.

Prawn vadai

MAKES 12

The one and only time I have been struck by food sickness in Sri Lanka was with a trio of vadai, a variety of lentil-based street food snacks, and I have no one to blame but myself. We were on our way to Kandy on a screamingly hot day. I am a little prone to car sickness, which I always think can be cured by constant snacking, so we made a pit stop for some vadai. They had a whiff of slightly rank coconut oil about them, but despite my suspicions I ate them. Greed outweighed sense, not for the first time, and I paid the price. All this aside, I still never refuse a vadai. A deep-fried snack should always be welcomed. Our version is based on the idea of the famous isso vadai, which sees small prawns stuck onto a disc of vadai and deep-fried, lined up and looking a little corpse-like. Here we use large prawns, dipped and protected in a cloud of vadai-ish batter.

- 12 large prawns (shrimps), shells on
- 12 long bamboo skewers
- neutral oil, for frying
- besan flour, for dusting
- salt flakes, to serve
- lime cheeks, to serve
- a generous sprinkle of White curry powder (page 26), Fermented chilli sauce (page 62), or Lunu dehi mayonnaise (page 35), to serve

BATTER

- 125 g (4½ oz) skinned urud dhal
- 125 g (4½ oz) red lentils
- 125 g (4½ oz) red onion, roughly chopped
- 25 g (1 oz) Maldive fish
- 10 g (⅓ oz) dried red chillies, roughly chopped
- 5 g (⅕ oz) long green chillies, roughly chopped
- 4 g (⅛ oz) salt flakes
- 3 g (1⁄10 oz) picked curry leaves

To make the batter, soak the urud dhal and the lentils together in water overnight; they don't need to go in the fridge. Use at least twice as much water as you have lentils, as they suck up quite a lot.

The next day, strain the lentils and transfer to a blender along with the rest of the ingredients. To make the batter, blitz the ingredients, slowly adding about 500 ml (17 fl oz) of water to form a batter. It doesn't need to be super smooth and should still be a little thick. Transfer to a bowl and let it sit overnight in the fridge to ferment.

To prepare your prawns, remove the middle shell, leaving the head and tail on. From the head, carefully use tweezers or a toothpick or some such thing to pull out the intestinal tract. Now, the next step is a question of looks really; if you want nice straight ones like you see here, you will need to carefully thread a skewer from the head to the tail down the back of the prawn. If you are happy with curly prawns, skip this step.

Use a deep fryer or fill a wide-based saucepan with about 4 cm (1½ in) of oil and heat to 180°C (360°F). Dust your prawns with besan flour and then, in batches, dip them in the batter, making sure to cover all of them well. Fry for about 3 minutes each, until the batter is cooked and crisp. The prawns will drop to the bottom of whatever you are frying in and will stick, so care must be taken. As they are ready, place the prawns on a wire rack and sprinkle with a good amount of salt. If you have used skewers, carefully remove them so as not to startle your guests with a bamboo stick in their mouths.

Serve while hot with lime cheeks on the side. If you are using curry powder, sprinkle this on top with the salt; otherwise, serve with either a small bowl of fermented chilli sauce or lunu dehi mayonnaise.

NOTE The batter needs to be started 2 days ahead to allow for soaking and fermenting.

Kangaroo pan rolls

MAKES 40

If you don't yet know about pan rolls then welcome, they are one of the greatest short eats of the island. A spicy filling is wrapped in a delicate crepe-like pancake, crumbed and then deep-fried, giving a delicious spicy mouthful with an intriguingly delightful texture. The fillings are generally either minced (ground) meat or some sort of vegetarian mix, the staples we served at LFS being a beef version and a potato and moru chilli one. But of course, the filling potentials are far vaster than this. I would put a slightly curried rabbit and carrot version on for Easter as an ode to the bunny, and also did a duck version scented with star anise and orange (you could try this with any leftover duck padre curry, page 189). At LFS, this version was our most regular addition though, and came about when we first started to slip more Australian ingredients onto the menu. Kangaroo meat is a little overlooked – it can be an unforgiving animal, as most of it is so lean. Minced and spiced though, we discovered, works perfectly here.

Fermented chilli sauce (page 62), to serve

KANGAROO FILLING

- 70 g (2½ oz) coconut oil
- 1.7 kg (3 lb 12 oz) coarsely minced (ground) kangaroo
- 340 g (12 oz) brown onion, finely diced
- 35 g (¼ oz) finely chopped garlic
- 35 g (1¼ oz) finely chopped ginger
- 35 g (1¼ oz) chilli powder
- 30 g (1 oz) Brown curry powder (page 27)
- 75 g (2¾ oz) tomato paste (concentrated puree)
- salt flakes and freshly ground black pepper
- 12 green bird's eye chillies, finely chopped
- 340 g (12 oz) celery, finely diced

To make the kangaroo filling, begin by browning off the meat. Heat half the coconut oil in a frying pan over a high heat and add the kangaroo in batches, cooking and stirring until well browned and breaking up any large clumps. Cook each batch for about 15 minutes to ensure the mix is dry and liquid free. Transfer each batch to a colander over a bowl to drain while you fry off the rest.

Melt the remaining coconut oil in a wide-based saucepan over a medium heat, add the onion, garlic and ginger and cook, stirring occasionally, for 4–5 minutes, until the onion has softened. Add the chilli and curry powders and the tomato paste and cook, stirring, for another minute or so until the curry powder starts to catch on the bottom of the pan. Add the kangaroo and season well with salt and pepper, then stir thoroughly to combine.

Add the fresh chilli and cook for another 2 minutes, then stir in the celery. Remove from the heat and have a taste – there should be a substantial hit of chilli heat, with the gentler spices coming through from the curry powder and a little crunch of celery. The mixture should be dry and almost a bit sticky. Set aside to cool to room temperature, then place in the fridge to chill a little.

To make the pancakes, sift the flour into a mixing bowl and add the salt. Whisk together the milk, eggs and 100 ml (3½ fl oz) of water in a jug. Gradually whisk the milk mixture into the flour, taking care to avoid any lumps forming. Once you have a nice smooth batter, vigorously whisk for another minute or so, then let it rest at room temperature for 30 minutes. (Alternatively, place all the ingredients in a blender and blitz until smooth.)

Now it's time to test your pancake-making skills. If you are using a non-stick pan you will not need any oil; if not, use a bit of paper towel dipped in oil to season your pan between pancakes.

Heat a 20 cm (8 in) non-stick frying pan or crepe pan over a medium heat, pour in around 45 ml (1½ fl oz) of batter and swirl it around to evenly cover the base, forming a nice, thin pancake. Cook for 1–2 minutes until only just about cooked through – the top should not be too sticky to touch but you also don't want the pancake to have any colour. Slide the pancake out of the pan and onto a tray with the more cooked side on the bottom. As you cook the pancakes, make sure to stack them up the same way. This stage is the trickiest to monitor. If you cook the pancakes too much

PANCAKES

- 600 g (1 lb 5 oz) plain (all-purpose) flour
- 12 g (½ oz) cooking salt
- 960 ml (32½ fl oz) full-cream (whole) milk
- 8 eggs
- vegetable oil, for pan-frying (optional)

FOR CRUMBING & FRYING

- 100 g (3½ oz) plain (all-purpose) flour
- 5 eggs
- 100 ml (3½ fl oz) full-cream (whole) milk
- 450 g (1 lb) coarse breadcrumbs (I like panko crumbs)
- vegetable oil, for deep-frying
- salt flakes

they will crack and not hold together when rolled; if you don't cook them enough they will stick together in the stack and be hard to separate. This will become fairly easy to get the hang of once you are actually doing it, and the recipe does allow for some mistakes.

Once all your pancakes are cooked you can start the filling and rolling (see the step-by-step images).

Place one pancake flat in front of you, again with the more cooked side down. Use a spoon to shape about 50 g (1¾ oz) of the filling into a log shape and place it in the middle of the bottom third of the pancake. Fold up the bottom so it covers the filling, fold in the two sides, then snugly but not super tightly roll it up to form a log (like a large spring roll). The pancake should be soft and sticky enough to hold itself together once rolled.

Set aside, seam side down, and repeat with the remaining pancakes and filling to make 40 rolls.

Wipe down the bench and set up a crumbing station.

Tip the flour in a bowl; whisk together the eggs and milk in a second bowl; and place the breadcrumbs in a third bowl. Have a clean tray or platter handy to put the crumbed rolls on.

Gently dust each roll in flour, shaking off the excess, then coat in the egg mixture, allowing the excess to drip off. Finally, coat the rolls in the breadcrumbs. Place on the clean tray or platter. At this stage, the rolls can be kept in the fridge for a few days or frozen to fry later.

Have a little clean, then get ready for frying.

Pour vegetable oil into a large heavy-based saucepan to a depth of 4–6 cm (1½–2½ in) – the oil should come no more than two-thirds of the way up the pan. Place over a high heat and heat to 170°C (340°F). If you don't have a thermometer you can check by dropping a few breadcrumbs into the oil; if they sizzle immediately, the oil is ready.

Working in small batches, fry the rolls for 5–6 minutes until they are a dark golden-brown colour, gently swishing them around so they cook evenly. Lift them out with a slotted spoon and drain on a wire rack. Season well with salt flakes. Give the oil a moment to heat up again before you fry the next batch.

Pan rolls are ready to be eaten when hot and go nicely with some Fermented chilli sauce. They can also be left for a few hours and served at room temperature. Alternatively they can be reheated in an oven for serving later.

NOTES If you are having trouble with your pancake batter you may need to make it slightly thicker or thinner. If you do add more flour or water, let the batter rest again before cooking with it.

If you find you are getting too many tears in your pancakes, cut some of the less perfect ones into quarters and place a piece in the middle of each whole pancake to reinforce it before rolling.

Patties

MAKES ENOUGH PASTRY FOR 20 PATTIES

And here we are, again looking at another very fine deep-fried street food snack, this one suspiciously empanada-like. And so it is, a flaky pastry parcel adapted from the time of the Portuguese on the island to contain spicy Lanky flavours. Within this pastry we can be free and easy with fillings. The Kangaroo pan roll mince would work (page 137), as would some seeni sambol (page 36) or any of the jaffle fillings (pages 91–2). All you need is a spicy, relatively dry morsel of something something that can then easily become a patty filling. Here are a few that we have had on the menu.

- 1 egg
- 20 ml (¾ fl oz) full-cream (whole) milk
- vegetable oil, for deep-frying
- salt flakes

PASTRY

- 400 g (14 oz) plain (all-purpose) flour
- 4 g (⅛ oz) baking powder
- 3 g (1⁄10 oz) cooking salt
- 80 g (2¾ oz) unsalted butter, chilled and diced
- 100 ml (3½ fl oz) coconut cream
- 2 egg yolks

For the pastry, you can either use a food processor or make it by hand; the method will be the same. Combine the flour, baking powder and salt in a bowl, then mix through the butter until it resembles fine breadcrumbs.

Lightly whisk together the coconut cream, egg yolks and 40 ml (1¼ fl oz) of water, then slowly add to the dry ingredients and mix or pulse until just combined.

Turn out the dough onto a floured bench and gently knead until it just comes together in a ball. Flatten the dough into a disc (this will make it easier to roll later), then wrap in plastic wrap and rest in the fridge for at least a few hours, or preferably overnight. The pastry can also be frozen for storage.

When it comes to rolling out the dough, a pasta machine is very useful, but of course you can do it by hand. This pastry has quite a lot of fat in it so it will be relatively easy to work with and should only need dusting with a little extra flourto prevent sticking.

Working in batches, roll out the dough to an even 3 mm (⅛ in) thickness, then cut it into discs using a 10 cm (4 in) round pastry cutter. Re-roll your scraps as you go to get the 20 rounds needed. Place your pastry rounds on a tray between layers of baking paper and keep them cool in the fridge. When you are ready to wrap your patties, take out small batches of pastry rounds as you go. You will probably have pastry left over; this can be rolled into a ball, stored in the fridge and reused.

Now, make your chosen filling (see options overleaf), then set aside to cool completely, and come back to this point when you're ready to make your patties.

Once the mixture has cooled, take about 1 tablespoon (25 g/¾ oz) of the filling, form it into a log shape and set it aside on a tray. Repeat until all the mix is divided and ready.

Whisk the egg and milk together to make an egg wash.

To make your patties, place a round of pastry on the bench in front of you, take one of the bits of filling and put it along the middle of the pastry. Lightly brush a little egg wash around the edge of half the pastry round. Gently fold the pastry over the filling to form a semi-circle, and lightly press down to flatten a little. Seal the edges and crimp with a fork, then transfer to a clean tray lined with baking paper and place in the fridge. Repeat with the remaining pastry and filling, adding each patty to the tray in the fridge as you go. You can stack them in two layers, but make sure you separate them with a piece of baking paper.

At this stage, the patties can be kept in the fridge for a few days or frozen to fry later.

Pour vegetable oil into a large heavy-based saucepan to a depth of 4–6 cm (1½–2½ in) (the oil should come no more than two-thirds of the way up the pan). Place over a high heat and heat to 170°C (340°F). If you don't have a thermometer you can check by dipping the edge of a patty into the oil; if it sizzles immediately, the oil is ready.

Working in small batches, fry the patties for 4–5 minutes or until they are a dark golden-brown colour, turning them halfway through and gently swishing them around so they cook evenly. Lift them out with a slotted spoon and drain on a wire rack. Season well with salt flakes. Give the oil a moment to heat up again before you fry the next batch.

The patties are now ready to serve, and best eaten hot immediately. The pork and pea ones would be good with a little Fermented chilli sauce (page 62), but the mozzarella ones are perfect as is.

Pork and pea

MAKES 20 PATTIES

What a fine combination this is, both for alliteration and flavour – spicy minced (ground) pork with a fresh pop of peas.

- 15 g (½ oz) ghee
- 5 g (⅕ oz) mustard seeds
- 3 g (⅒ oz) fennel seeds
- 4 g (⅛ oz) picked curry leaves
- 150 g (5½ oz) diced brown onion
- 12 g (½ oz) chopped garlic
- 12 g (½ oz) chopped ginger
- 1–2 long green chillies, chopped
- 8 g (¼ oz) Brown curry powder (page 27)
- 8 g (¼ oz) fenugreek seeds, roasted and ground
- 200 g (7 oz) minced (ground) pork
- 120 g (4½ oz) fresh or frozen peas, blanched
- salt flakes and ground white pepper

Warm the ghee in a wide-based saucepan over a medium heat. Add in the mustard and fennel seeds, and curry leaves and cook them for 1 minute, until the spices are popping and the leaves fried.

Add in the onion, garlic, ginger and chilli and cook this off, stirring, for about 3 minutes, until the onion has completely softened. Add the curry powder and fenugreek and season well.

Add in the pork, increase the heat to high and cook, mashing up the mince, for about 6 minutes, until the filling is nicely mixed, cooked and browned.

Add in the peas and mix well, then remove from the heat. Your mix should be a little sticky and dry. Have a taste and season if needed, then set aside to cool. Once the mix is cool you can then fill and cook your patties, using 25 g (1 oz) mix per patty.

Mozzarella, buffalo curd and katta sambol

MAKES 20 PATTIES

Cheesy and gooey and super fiery from the sambol, this is one of my favourite patty fillings. Use that weird firm yellow supermarket mozzarella. And see the roti recipe on page 98 for more information about buffalo curd and potential substitutes.

- 200 g (7 oz) firm mozzarella, cut into 5 mm (¼ in) dice
- 200 g (7 oz) buffalo curd, cut into 5 mm (¼ in) dice
- 100 g (3½ oz) Katta sambol (page 34)
- salt flakes and freshly ground black pepper

Combine all the ingredients in a bowl and season with lots of pepper and a little salt. Fill and cook your patties using 25 g (1 oz) mix per patty.

Fried meat sambol

MAKES 20 PATTIES

This sambol works so well in the patties, as it's nice and dry and strongly flavoured and aromatic giving you a moreish mouthful. When you look at the recipe for this sambol you will note I speak of a fish and vegetarian version as well; these would work equally as well bundled inside this flaky pastry house.

- 500 g (1 lb 2 oz) Fried meat sambol (page 41)

Fill and cook your patties using 25 g mix (1 oz) per patty.

Hot butter cuttlefish

SERVES 2–4

Although salt and pepper squid is a Cantonese dish, we have adopted it so thoroughly into Australian culture that it's a rare pub, rural or otherwise, that wouldn't have it on the menu. I feel this dish – HBC, as it's fondly known – has followed a similar trajectory, from a Chinese recipe that has been adapted to become a modern Sri Lankan classic. And then I've gone and messed with the dish to create yet another version. But like the original, it's still served hot, laden with chilli and hints of sweetness, a very fine starter to get you going.

- 750 ml (25½ fl oz) vegetable oil, for deep-frying
- 160 g (5½ oz) cleaned cuttlefish, cut into triangular pieces about 6 cm (2½ in) at their longest edge
- 25 g (1 oz) fine rice flour, for dusting
- 2 long red chillies, split down the middle from top to bottom, seeds scraped and discarded

BATTER

- 125 g (4½ oz) fine rice flour
- 1 teaspoon coconut oil, in liquid form
- 1 teaspoon vegetable oil
- 1 teaspoon white vinegar
- 1 teaspoon bicarbonate of soda (baking soda)
- 125 ml (4 fl oz) soda water, cold

HOT BUTTER AND BITS

- splash of vegetable oil
- ½ medium red onion, cut into 6 wedges
- 3 spring onions (scallions), cut into 6 cm (2½ in) lengths, including all the green part
- 1 small banana chilli, halved, seeds removed and sliced diagonally into 5 mm (¼ in) strips
- 10 g (⅓ oz) finely chopped garlic
- 140 g (5 oz) Hot butter (page 57), cut into small chunks
- 3 g (1⁄10 oz) caster (superfine) sugar
- fish sauce

To make the batter, place the flour into a bowl along with all other ingredients except the soda water. Use a whisk to combine, then slowly add the soda, whisking as you go to form a smooth batter. This batter is best made just before you want to use it. If it's made too soon it will separate (if this happens, carefully whisk it back together).

Pour the vegetable oil into a large heavy-based saucepan to a depth of 4–6 cm (1½–2½ in) – the oil should come no more than two-thirds of the way up the pan). Place over a high heat and heat to 180°C (350°F). If you don't have a thermometer you can check by dropping a little batter into the oil; if it sits on the top and immediately starts to sizzle, the oil is ready.

Very lightly dust the cuttlefish pieces in rice flour, then use a spoon to dip them into the batter, making sure every piece is coated in a nice layer of batter.

Working in batches so you don't overcrowd the pan, use the spoon to carefully drop the battered cuttlefish into the hot oil. Use a slotted spoon to gently jiggle them around so they don't stick to the bottom of the pan or each other. Cook for 2–3 minutes, until the batter is super crispy. Lift them out and drain on a wire rack. Give the oil a moment to heat up again before you fry the next batch. Once all the cuttlefish is cooked, fry your chilli halves in the oil until they start to soften and darken, about 1 minute. Set these aside on the wire rack along with the cuttlefish.

For the hot butter and bits, heat the vegetable oil in a wok over a high heat. Add the onion, spring onion and banana chilli and cook, stirring and tossing, for 2 minutes, until slightly softened. Add in the garlic and let it cook for a minute before adding the hot butter and caster sugar.

Once the hot butter has melted and is sizzling, add the fried cuttlefish and toss for another minute or so to coat and combine.

Season with fish sauce and serve immediately.

Chickpea flour fried fish wings

MAKES AS MANY FISH WINGS AS YOU WANT

When you work in a restaurant and get a whole fish, it's usually the fillet that gets served, with the rest relegated to scraps and staff food. Lucky for the staff, I say, as the wings of a fish, and its collar, are probably my favourite parts. The wings have a bit of cartilage-like bone to chew on, and the flesh is fatty and unctuous. I think now though, people are more inclined to embrace these bits. When we would put wings on as a special, they were very quickly ordered (the only problem being that there are only two wings per fish). We didn't make a tricky batter for them, we just dusted them in a combination of seasoned chickpea and rice flours and served with any number of sauces, depending on the mood. The recipe below is in ratios rather than specific amounts, giving you the freedom to cook as many or as few wings as you desire with whatever type of fish you choose. Perhaps you have filleted a large fish and have spare wings on hand or, more likely, you have gone to a fishmonger to buy them specifically. This is more of a how-to than a proper recipe.

- chickpea (besan) flour
- fine rice flour
- vegetable oil, for frying
- fish wings, at room temperature
- salt flakes

ALL AMOUNTS BELOW ARE FOR ONE MEDIUM WING:

HOT BUTTER

- 5 ml (⅛ fl oz) cooking oil
- 10 g (⅓ oz) finely chopped garlic
- 70 g (2½ oz) Hot butter (page 57)
- 3 g (1/10 oz) sugar
- 15 ml (½ fl oz) fish sauce

WHITE CURRY POWDER

- 5 g (⅕ oz) White curry powder (page 26)
- lime cheeks, to serve
- Fermented chilli sauce (page 62)

FERMENTED CHILLI

- 5 g (⅕ oz) Fermented chilli powder (page 63)
- Fermented chilli sauce (page 62)
- lime cheeks, to serve

TAMARIND SAUCE

- 50 g (1¾ oz) tamarind sauce (page 159)

Sift and combine the two flours in equal measure, adding salt flakes to taste.

Have an appropriately sized saucepan or wok that will hold the wings of your choice. The shape of a wok is ideal for this. Fill with enough oil to submerge your wings and heat to 180°C (360°F).

Place the seasoned flours on a plate and heavily dust your wings on all sides. Working one at a time, gently lower the wing into the oil and fry until golden and cooked through; you may need to turn it at some stage. One 440 g (15½ oz) wing will take about 6–7 minutes to cook.

Carefully remove the wing from the oil and transfer it onto a wire rack. Immediately season it with salt but let it rest for about 5 minutes and then use one of the suggestions below to serve.

HOT BUTTER

Heat the oil in a small saucepan, add the garlic and fry until fragrant and just cooked, about a minute, then add in the hot butter to melt. Once the butter has melted, season with the sugar and fish sauce and pour it straight over the wing to serve.

WHITE CURRY POWDER

Once you have seasoned the fish wing with salt, generously sprinkle with white curry powder. Serve with lime cheeks and fermented chilli sauce.

FERMENTED CHILLI

Once you have seasoned the fish wing with salt, generously sprinkle over fermented chilli powder. Serve with a side of fermented chilli sauce and lime cheeks.

TAMARIND SAUCE

Heat the sauce and pour it over the cooked wing.

NOTE One small wing (around 180 g/6½ oz) will need about 10 g (⅓ oz) of seasoned mixed flour; one medium wing (around 440 g/15½ oz) will need about 20 g (¾ oz) of seasoned mixed flour.

Devilled chicken livers with fermented chilli and kithul

SERVES 4–6

Doesn't saying 'devilled something' just sound good? It's one of the great Sri Lankan dish descriptors, as versatile as the head wobble, a term that can be put in front of almost anything and simply means hot. Generally, devilled dishes are dry fried or only slightly saucy in a sticky kind of way, and are a medium-sized snack that seems specifically designed for you to have a fork in one hand and a drink in the other. This version sees seared, slightly charred livers coated in sweet and hot flavours. It's a little bit rich and a little bit juicy.

- 200 g (7 oz) whole chicken livers
- 40 g (1½ oz) ghee, plus 20 g (¾ oz) extra
- 4 g (⅛ oz) picked curry leaves
- 100 g (3½ oz) red onion, sliced thinly with the grain
- 2 long red chillies, cut into thin rounds
- 30 g (1 oz) ginger, julienned
- 60 ml (2 fl oz) Fermented chilli sauce (page 62)
- 20 ml (¾ fl oz) kithul
- salt flakes and freshly ground black pepper
- 2 lime cheeks, to serve

Separate the two lobes of each chicken liver, then use a sharp knife to remove any sinew or blood clots. Season both sides with a little salt.

Place a wok or large frying pan over a high heat, then add 40 g (1½ oz) of the ghee. Once it's hot and shimmering, use tongs to gently place the livers in the wok to sear in a single layer. Give them about 30 seconds, turn them, then give them another 30 seconds before removing them from the heat. Take your wok off the heat but leave the ghee in the base.

Cut the liver pieces into bite-sized morsels; the smaller lobe in half, the larger in two or three pieces. Set aside.

Place your wok back over a medium heat and add in the curry leaves. Once they've started to crisp, add in the onion, chilli and ginger and cook, stirring, for about 3 minutes, until the onion starts to caramelise. Season a little here.

Add the fermented chilli sauce, the kithul and extra ghee along with the fish sauce and some more seasoning, then stir to combine and have a taste. It should be hot and a little buttery, with a nice amount of sweetness balanced with the salt.

Add the livers back to this saucy mix and cook everything together for another minute, then serve hot from the wok with the lime cheeks on the side.

NOTE If you can, source good hand-picked whole livers for this dish as this will give you the best quality; you want them to be nice, firm and whole and not squishy.

Moru chilli chicken

SERVES 2–4

This dish is based on that excellent Sichuan dish of deep-fried pieces of chicken, wok-cooked with so many chillies it looks scary. It came about both because of my deep admiration for the original dish, one of the exceptions to my non-chicken-eating rule, and my deep love of moru chillies. They are perfect here. Not only do they bring the heat, they also add a delicious salty sour flavour. And if you look at the ingredients of the traditional Sichuan version – ginger, garlic, spring onions, dried chilli – it's a fairly generic 'Asian' base that can easily be prodded into the direction of Sri Lanka.

- 280 g (10 oz) chicken thigh fillets, skin on
- 100 ml (3½ fl oz) shaoxing rice wine
- vegetable oil, for frying
- 5 g (⅕ oz) moru chillies, cut into 1 cm (½ in) pieces
- 5 g (⅕ oz) picked curry leaves
- 50 g (1¾ oz) spring onions (scallions), cut into thin rounds
- 20 g (¾ oz) ginger, julienned
- 20 g (¾ oz) garlic cloves, finely chopped
- 1 long red chilli, cut into thin rounds
- 12 g (½ oz) small dried chillies
- 60 g (2 oz) Moru chilli sambol (page 37)
- 2 sprigs of coriander (cilantro), roots and stalks washed and finely chopped, leaves picked
- 20 g (¾ oz) Chinese celery, finely chopped

BATTER

- 125 g (4½ oz) fine rice flour
- 4 g (⅛ oz) chilli powder
- 4 g (⅛ oz) paprika
- 2 g (1/16 oz) salt flakes
- 1 teaspoon coconut oil, in liquid forn
- 1 teaspoon vegetable oil
- 1 teaspoon white vinegar
- 1 teaspoon bicarbonate of soda (baking soda)
- 125 g (4½ oz) soda water, cold

Cut the chicken thighs into a 1.5 cm (½ in) dice. Place in a mixing bowl, pour over the shao tsing and let this sit for about an hour.

Just before you are ready to start, make your batter. Place the rice flour into a bowl and sift in the chilli powder and paprika. Add all remaining batter ingredients except the soda water. Use a whisk to combine, then slowly add the water, whisking as you go to form a smooth batter. This batter is best made just before you want to use it. If it's made too soon it will separate (if this happens, carefully whisk it back together).

Strain any excess liquid off the chicken then place all the chicken pieces into the bowl with the batter.

Fill a wok or large saucepan with enough oil to deep-fry and heat to 180°C (360°F). Use a spoon to gently lower in the chicken pieces; you may need to do this in batches. Swizzle them around in the oil so they separate, and cook for about 8 minutes, until they are just cooked through. Remove from the oil and transfer to a wire rack.

Strain your oil and set aside; it can be re-used for cooking at some stage in your kitchen life.

Heat a wok over a high heat, add a splash of oil and then add in the moru chillies. Swirl them around for a moment before adding in the curry leaves. Once the leaves start to crisp, add in the spring onions, ginger and garlic. Cook this down for about a minute, then add in the chillies and moru chilli sambol.

Once the base is looking good, add the chicken pieces. Toss to combine a few times to let everything mingle properly before throwing in the chopped coriander (roots and stalks) and the celery. Give this a final toss to combine and then remove from the heat.

Serve immediately garnished with the coriander leaves.

NOTE If you want to cook this recipe yet don't have time to make the moru chilli sambol (which would be sad), you can do without – it will only be slightly lacking.

GENEROUSLY

SIZED

EATS

INCLUDING CURRIES AND A BURYANI

There are so many ways to approach a proper sit-down meal but my preferred option, whatever the cuisine, is a table laden with different dishes, varying colours and textures, each celebrating a particular flavour. I much prefer being able to pick and choose what I put on my plate myself – almost to the point of obsessiveness, as I can become quite particular about what I want, where and how much. Too many things or too full a plate can upset me. Putting aside this slight quirk of mine, the main idea of eating like this (the variety, not my strange plate habits) is very much in tune with the way most Asian meals are constructed. All dishes are separate, with distinct flavours, and all have a purpose.

Some recipes in this chapter are suited to this way of eating – more substantial plates that work best as part of a meal alongside some sides, a sambol and maybe some rice. The kind of dishes that you prepare when you have time on your hands and want to cook for people you love. But of course, you can't eat like this every day – who has that much time? Also, you would get very full. And so we have also included some recipes here that are one plate beauties, some easier for a mid-week meal and others still a bit more labour intensive.

In among this mix we have some curry dishes that lean towards the more traditional way, and others that take Sri Lankan flavours and put them elsewhere, like in a pasta dish. As we have said, there are no real rules, and I am assuming if you are reading this you are a grown-up with your own ideas and can therefore figure out how you would like to cook and serve the delights from this chapter.

Roasted king prawns

This method for preparing and cooking prawns is blatant thievery from Muu and appears in his excellent cookbook, *ester*. It is a very clever way of dealing with these delightful crustaceans as it caters to those who like eating with their fingers, sucking head juices and getting messy and tactile with shells, as well as for those of a more delicate sensibility who prefer to gracefully ease the meat from the shell using a knife and fork. And everyone knows cooking on the bone or shell is much more sensible, both for extra flavour and for protecting delicate flesh.

What you have below is a method for preparing and cooking these beauties without giving you an exact amount of prawns. Maybe you are just cooking some for yourself, perhaps you are preparing them for a hot dinner date or maybe you're having a party? Only you can answer that question ... There are also three different sauce options overleaf so really, it's a bit of a choose your own adventure.

- large king prawns (shrimp)
- 10 ml (¼ fl oz) grapeseed oil per prawn
- salt flakes

To prepare the prawns, hold one flat in your hand with the tail towards you. Use kitchen scissors to cut the shell from the tail along the length of the belly, just above the feelers, to the start of the head. Cut again in this manner along the back. Peel this top half of the shell from the body, leaving the head and tail in place. Now, cut along the length of the head from the base to the tip so you can pull the head open, butterflying it. You should be able to remove the vein by pulling it from the top. Repeat with all the prawns. (If this sounds too confusing, *ester* has pictures, but I don't think I'm allowed to tell you to buy it ...). Basically, you want to end up with a prawn that has a butterflied head and half the shell still covering one side to protect the flesh while you are cooking.

TO COOK

Preheat the oven to 200°C (390°F). Place a heavy-based ovenproof frying pan, big enough to fit the prawns in a single layer, into the oven and leave it in there for about 10 minutes, until it is smoking hot.

Carefully remove the pan from the oven, place it over a high heat and lay the prawns, shell side down, into the pan. Pour in the oil and press the prawns flat with a fish spatula for a moment. Season the flesh with salt flakes and return the pan to the oven for 2–3 minutes, until the prawns are just barely cooked through.

Remove the pan from the oven, pour over the warmed sauce of your choice, give the pan a little jiggle to introduce them to each other and then serve.

Roasted king prawn sauces

Black pepper and coconut

MAKES 400 ML (13½ FL OZ)

This is a thick sauce, a little bit creamy but laden with pepper.

- 16 g (½ oz) cracked black pepper, coarse
- 60 g (2 oz) ghee
- 6 g (⅕ oz) picked curry leaves
- 200 g (7 oz) eschalots, finely diced
- 25 g (1 oz) garlic
- 10 g (⅓ oz) jaggery, grated or chopped
- 250 ml (8½ fl oz) coconut cream
- 10 ml (¼ fl oz) fish sauce
- salt flakes

Dry toast the black pepper in a saucepan over a medium heat until it's very aromatic and a little bit smoky, about a minute or so. Add the ghee, let it melt, then add the curry leaves and allow to fry for a little.

Add in the eschalot, garlic and some salt to season, and cook, stirring occasionally, until softened, about 2 minutes.

Add the jaggery and, once it has melted, add in the coconut cream and 50 ml (1¾ fl oz) of water. Cook this over a low heat until you see the sauce split, about 20 minutes. Keep cooking for another few minutes to allow the coconut to caramelise.

Add in another 190 ml (6½ fl oz) of water, bring to the boil, season with the fish sauce, then serve.

Pepperberry

MAKES 400 ML (13½ FL OZ)

Pepperberry is powerful in both flavour and looks, so this makes for a tasty, lurid-looking sauce.

4 g (⅛ oz) pepperberry
6 g (⅕ oz) black peppercorns
2 g (1/16 oz) salt flakes
35 ml (1¼ fl oz) grapeseed oil
3 g (1/10 oz) picked curry leaves
250 g (9 oz) red onion, finely diced
25 g (1 oz) garlic, finely chopped
50 ml (1 fl oz) arrack
300 ml (10 fl oz) chicken stock
juice of 1 lime

Using a mortar and pestle, pound both the pepperberry and pepper along with the salt until fine. Set aside.

Heat the oil in a medium saucepan over a gentle heat and fry the curry leaves off for a moment until crisp before adding in the onion and garlic. Cook for about 3 minutes, stirring occasionally, until softened.

Add in the pepperberry mix, give it a few turns around the pan and then deglaze the pan with the arrack. Let it sizzle for a moment before adding in the chicken stock. Turn the heat up and bring the mix to a boil before turning the heat down to gently reduce until it thickens, about 12 minutes. The sauce should be thick and flavourful.

Season with a little lime, to serve.

Caramelised tamarind

MAKES 400 ML (13½ FL OZ)

This is a delightfully sweet and sour sauce.

50 ml (1¾ fl oz) coconut oil
3 g (1/10 oz) picked curry leaves
180 g (6½ oz) red onion, finely diced
salt flakes
40 g (1½ oz) jaggery, grated or chopped
25 g (10 fl oz) tamarind

PASTE

2 cm (¾ in) off the base of 2 stalks of lemon grass
10 g (⅓ oz) garlic cloves
10 g (⅓ oz) ginger, roughly chopped
30 g (1 oz) red chillies, roughly chopped
80 g (2¾ oz) red onion, roughly chopped
3 g (1/10 oz) black peppercorns
7 g (¼ oz) chilli powder

Place all of the paste ingredients into a blender and blitz until smooth.

Place a medium saucepan over a gentle heat and add in the coconut oil. Once it's hot, add in the paste, turn the heat down and cook gently until it splits, about 10 minutes.

Once it has split, turn the heat up, add in the curry leaves to fry a little, then add the onions. Return the heat to medium and continue cooking until the onion softens, about 5 minutes. Season with a little salt.

Add in the jaggery and tamarind and cook for 2 minutes before adding in 1 litre (34 fl oz) of water. Cook the sauce for about half an hour, until it reduces and thickens by about half. It should start looking a little shiny.

Sauce is ready to serve.

MUD CRABS (AND HOW TO EAT THEM)

I know serving whole crabs can be a great divider among humans, largely because of the preparing and eating. I think there are very few people who would reject a delicate little crab toast (page 114), for example, but many would think twice about getting involved in a meal where you have to extract the flesh yourself. And I do understand those who refuse it on the grounds of it being messy and too much hard work. I get it, really I do, sometimes it's just not the right moment. The luxury of spooning the delicate flesh of some pre-picked crabmeat is a true delight, but in my mind this is equal to the moment when you gently pull the hind leg of the crab in just the right way to reveal a plump, perfectly cooked mound of flesh just barely holding onto the shell, like the perfect oceanic lollipop to slip in your mouth. And yes, mud crabs can be a bit expensive to buy, but also not really if you compare the cost to that of a slab of fancy meat.

The next hurdle most people face is feeling like they don't know how to prepare or cook a crab, but actually, the preparation is minimal, and the cooking super fast and simple. I say this knowing full well that despite the small oceans of crabs I have cooked in my life, I still squeal a little when faced with one of these moving beasts. As I prepare to chop it in half, I always pray to the crab gods in repentance.

The method here shows the crab in the simplest of sauces, with curry leaf butter, but it can easily be adapted to use either vadouvan (page 58) or hot butter (page 57). It is also delicious with any of the sauces suggested for the roasted prawns (page 157). Master the method of preparing and cooking your crab and soon there will be a world of flavours you can experiment with.

Mud crab with curry leaf butter

- 1 mud crab, between 1–1.5 kg (2 lb 3 oz–3 lb 5 oz)
- splash of neutral oil
- 4 large garlic cloves, finely chopped
- 5 g (⅕ oz) picked curry leaves
- 200 g (7 oz) Curry leaf butter (page 57)
- 2 g (1/16 oz) ground white pepper
- juice of 1 lime
- salt flakes

There are, of course, many ways to deal with a crab, but this is what I do. Place the mud crab in your freezer for about half an hour. This sends it to sleep a little, which makes the process of cutting it up nicer for both of you. Once it is sufficiently stilled, remove from the freezer and place the top shell down on a board with the large claws farthest from you. Take a heavy cleaver and swiftly cut your crab in half from the top down. Hold one half over a bowl and remove the top shell, pulling it from the underside flap. The top shell can be kept and cooked with your crab body for garnish, if you so desire. Regardless, be sure to use any juicy bits hiding in the crevices. Remove any of the feathery gills on the edge of the body and then cut the body in half again. Use either the back of your cleaver or a pestle to gently tap the large claw and the section below until it splits a little. Repeat with the other half and place the pieces of crab in the bowl with any reserved juices.

Warm a wok over a low heat and add in the oil, garlic and curry leaves. Season with a little salt. Cook this very gently, stirring, for about 3–4 minutes, until the garlic starts to colour.

Add in the crab and reserved juices and turn the heat up to high to get a bit of colour. Cook for a minute or so, then turn the crab halves and add in the butter of your choice, along with a splash of water.

Once the juicy bits have started to sizzle, place a lid over your wok and cook the crab for another 10–14 minutes. Turn and baste your crab pieces occasionally. Look for colour to tell if the crab is ready. It will quickly start turning orange, but to check if it's fully cooked, use a thin metal skewer to pierce the claw where you have cracked the shell. Leave the skewer in for a moment or two, then pull it out. If it's warm, the crab should be ready. Remove from the heat, add in the pepper and season with more salt if necessary and a bit of lime – only just enough to taste in the background.

Mix through and serve immediately with a carb of your choice.

AND HOW TO EAT IT...

First, some words of advice, and then pictures to help (these instructions are based on the luxury of having half a crab per person, and does apply to most crabs whether large or small).

Note – it's important to be prepared. Have a bowl for shells, a crab claw for picking and a crab cracker for getting into the claw. A pile of napkins is good to clean as you go, with a finger bowl scented with citrus waiting for you at the end. Also, I would never be ashamed of a crab bib.

Whichever way you look at it, eating crab is indeed a messy experience, but there are ways to do it in a sensible and delicate manner. It's just a matter of understanding the shell structure, so you know which direction to head in, and which bits you want to eat first. My first bit of advice is, although it's called eating with your hands, using your fingertips is all that's necessary, and a much more refined way to get involved. This won't prevent the inevitable juices dribbling from your hands to your elbows, but it is a start. I approach the crab by dividing it into three sections and deciding which I want to start with: the claw, the legs or the body. The crab claw offers great flesh-to-shell satisfaction, the smaller legs offer great sweetness but little sustenance, while the body itself offers the greatest flesh, but hidden, in hard to reach cavities.

With practice it will get easier and less messy – to the point where you may even be brave enough to do this in public.

The claw

I like to start here as it is the hardest shell to crack, so is best dealt with at the beginning, when you are feeling fresh. The claw offers an abundance of flesh, which will also help with immediate hunger pains, giving you the strength you need to go forward. The texture of the claw meat is more robust than the body and for some this is the pinnacle. This is where you will need to use your crab claw (to get into the crab claw ...) to crack open the shell. This part is eaten in two sections, the top of the claw and the arm of the claw.

The legs

This is where I go next, slowing to a more relaxed pace after the battle of the claw. I first pull away the three thin legs from the body. There's not much going on inside, but what's there is delicate and gentle. On a smaller crab you may just need to use your back teeth to gently chew along the flat side of each leg, sucking and extracting what flesh you can. If the legs are bigger, snap away a section in a slight twisting motion to reveal a thin stick of flesh inside. And then you get to my very favourite moment of crab eating, the hind leg, which is attached to the best bit, a mound of flesh almost like a knuckle. In one hand, hold the body of the crab and in the other, clasp the top bit of the hind leg where it joins the body. Gently wiggle this around a little and then carefully pull it away from the body. You will be left holding the leg attached to a perfect round of flesh, all wibbly and wobbly, soft and decadent. Before you eat this, please pause a moment to consider its glory. Dip it into the sauce and slowly savour the texture and flavour of this perfect piece of flesh. Then quietly chew on the rest of the hind leg which, though fleshless, should be juicy and flavourful. Feel free to pause a moment before you move on to the body.

The body

The body is a soft carapace filled with several cavities. You need go through each one, extracting the flesh and discarding the shell as you go. If you can, try to split this part open down the middle, like a book. If you are very lucky and the crab is cooked perfectly, you can just shake it and the flesh will fall out in pieces like a bountiful waterfall. You can eat as you go here, but my preferred technique is to pick the flesh into a mound onto my plate using the crab picker. I then wash my hands and reach for a spoon, scooping up this most delicate bit of the crab, along with the juices left on the plate. This also presents a fine opportunity for noodles, rice or bread to get involved to help you soak up all the juices.

Mussels in rassam

SERVES 2–4

A rassam is a sour soupy number, a thin tamarind-based broth with tempered spices, maybe some vegetables, perhaps some lentils, often seasoned with a lot of pepper. In Sri Lanka it's often served pre-meal in a glass or cup, to whet the appetite and awaken the tastebuds, or it's served alongside thoasai and dosa for dipping, or with some rice. It is versatile and quick, and oh so good for you. Here, it's turned into an easy meal, the broth prepared and the mussels gently simmered in it to open. All you need is some roti or rice on the side to mop up the juices.

- 100 g (3½ oz) French green lentils
- 40 g (1½ oz) tamarind pulp
- 1 bunch coriander (cilantro), leaves picked and washed, to garnish, stems and root washed and finely chopped
- 15 g (½ oz) peeled ginger, finely chopped
- 15 g (½ oz) garlic cloves, finely chopped
- 100 g (3½ oz) ghee
- 4 g (⅛ oz) coriander seeds
- 1 g (1⁄32 oz) mustard seeds
- 1 g (1⁄32 oz) cumin seeds
- 3 g (1⁄10 oz) chilli powder
- 2 g (1⁄16 oz) turmeric powder
- 3 g (1⁄10 oz) picked curry leaves
- 150 g (5½ oz) cherry tomatoes, halved
- white pepper and salt flakes
- 1 kg (2 lb 3 oz) mussels

Place the lentils into a saucepan, generously cover with cold water and bring to a boil. Simmer for 2 minutes, then strain and set aside.

Next, prepare your tamarind. Soak the pulp in 70 ml (2¼ fl oz) boiling water for 30 minutes, then push it through a fine strainer. Set aside.

Use a mortar and pestle to grind the coriander stems and root, ginger and garlic into a paste; use a little salt to help with this. Set aside.

Place a wide-based saucepan with a lid, large enough to hold the mussels, over a medium heat and add in the ghee. Allow it to warm before adding in the spices. Stir and cook the spices for about 1 minute, until they start to toast and sizzle, then add in the curry leaves and fry them off for another 30 seconds or so.

Add the coriander paste and cook, stirring for another minute before adding in the tomatoes, then season well. Give the tomatoes a few moments in the pan before adding the tamarind, lentils and another 300 ml (10 fl oz) of water. Bring to a boil, then turn the heat down to very low and allow to gently cook for 10 minutes.

Have a taste and season a little more if needed. The flavour should be sour with a richness from the ghee, and I like it to be quite peppery. Add in your mussels, give everything a good stir, increase the heat to medium and put the lid on your saucepan. The mussels should cook fairly quickly, in around 3 minutes. You'll know they're done once they have mostly popped open (see Note).

Serve in a bowl, or straight from the pot if you desire, garnished with the coriander leaves.

NOTE Someone once started a dirty rumour that if a mollusc doesn't pop open when cooking, it is bad. This is not always the case. If you have an off mollusc, or shellfish, the smell is usually so distinctive it will be painfully apparent before you even cook it. Saying that, though, if you ever encounter an unopened shell in amongst the popped ones, use a fork to gently prise it open and have a gentle sniff. If it is bad, you will know immediately.

Pipis with Maldive fish XO and fried string hoppers

SERVES 4

Once we had invented our version of XO, the next step was to see how many things we could use it with, and this idea was the first. It's a Cantonese classic that has become a stalwart of the Australian dining scene. As I have said before, the base ingredients in Sri Lankan cooking often closely mirror those of Chinese cookery, you just need to add curry leaves to nudge it closer. The other revelation for us in this dish was using string hoppers instead of the usual rice vermicelli. Again, they are kind of the same. Both are noodles made with rice flour, but the string hoppers are steamed where the vermicelli is boiled. So in my mind, it's a short straight line to get from that classic dish to this version. You can make the string hoppers yourself if you have lots of spare time and want to learn a new skill – and, as it happens, I know there's a good recipe in *Lanka Food.* Otherwise you can buy them pre-made from a Sri Lankan grocer, or just use rice vermicelli instead. And please, make sure your molluscs are fully purged, as no one wants sand in their mouth.

- vegetable oil, for frying
- 12 string hoppers
- 30 g (1 oz) ghee
- 5 g (⅕ oz) picked curry leaves
- 100 g (3½ oz) red onion, thinly sliced with the grain
- 1 long red chilli, thinly sliced
- salt flakes
- 100 g (3½ oz) Maldive fish sambol (page 40)
- 10 g (⅓ oz) jaggery, grated or finely chopped
- 1 kg (2 lb 3 oz) vongole, pipis or small clams
- 30 ml (1 fl oz) arrack
- 100 ml (3½ oz) chicken stock or water

Pour about 1 cm (½ in) of oil in large, wide-based pan and heat until just before the oil starts to smoke. Gently place as many string hoppers into the pan as you can in a single layer, and shallow fry them in batches until golden and crisp. You will need to turn them midway. As they are ready, lay them on a wire rack.

Heat a wok over a high heat, then add in the ghee. Once the ghee is shimmering, add the curry leaves, stir, and then add the onion and chilli. Season with a little salt and cook for about 2 minutes, until the mix starts to colour.

Add in the Maldive fish sambol and the jaggery and give that at least a minute or so before adding in the clams. Toss to combine, then add the shao tsing. Let this reduce almost completely before adding in the stock or water, then place a lid or bowl over your wok and turn the heat down a little.

Give the clams another minute or so, then release the lid and give them a little stir and check them. Continue in this manner until nearly all of the clams have popped open. At this stage, use a large, slotted spoon to remove the clams from the wok into a heatproof bowl. (If you are feeling very industrious, use tongs, and remove the clams individually as they pop open. This may seem crazy, but it is actually a very proper way.)

Once the clams are all out, let the sauce keep bubbling over a high heat until it has reduced by almost half. Make sure to taste and check for seasoning as you go.

Arrange your string hoppers along the base of a large platter, spoon the clams on top and, once the sauce is ready, pour this over. Serve immediately.

NOTE If you can't find arrack, rice wine is a good substitute.

Curried pumpkin tortellini with moru chilli sambol

MAKES 40 TORTELLINI (5 PER PERSON FOR A STARTER OR 10 PER PERSON FOR A MAIN)

This dish was invented for one of our crab curry Sundays; for years, a monthly affair. The menu was an array of short eats followed by crab curry and all the accompaniments. We would base this ever-changing menu around whatever was taking our fancy at the time, often choosing to honour a cuisine from around the world. It was super fun designing the menus as it was our chance to experiment with non-traditional dishes. In fact, many of the recipes in this book were born from those menus. This one came about because Corentin had bought a pasta machine and was madly making doughs and rolling them at home, so I decided it was time for an Italian moment. Pumpkin-filled pasta is a bit of a classic in Italy, while a pumpkin curry is traditional to Sri Lanka, so combining them made sense to us, with the versatile kiri hodi (page 205) as the sauce. Adding the moru chilli sambol (page 37) on top with a drizzle of olive oil was the perfect finish, offering savoury and heat to cut through all those gentle, sweet flavours.

- **600 g peeled Kent pumpkin (winter squash), cut into 3 cm (1¼ in in) chunks**
- **10 g (⅓ oz) ghee, melted**
- **3 g (1/10 oz) Brown curry powder (page 27)**
- **480 ml (16 fl oz) strained Kiri hodi (page 205), warmed**
- **80 g (2¾ oz) Moru chilli sambol (page 37)**
- **olive oil, to drizzle**

PASTA

- **100 g (3½ oz) whole eggs**
- **2 egg yolks**
- **230 g (8 oz) 00 flour**
- **7 g (¼ oz) cooking salt**

NOTE Making your own pasta can be quite simple but, like all things, practice makes perfect and the more you begin to understand it the more you will discover there is to learn. And then of course, once it's made, the whole rolling process becomes just as important as the dough. And then there's the shaping technique ... This is the simplest of doughs with the briefest of methods; if you have your own way, please feel free to use it. If you are starting out I encourage you to research more thorough explanations than I have given here. Or just find some thin pre-made fresh pasta sheets and use those.

To make your pasta, first place your eggs and yolks in a small bowl and use a fork to break them up slightly. Place the flour and salt in a mixing bowl or straight onto a bench. Make a well in the centre and pour in the eggs. Use your fingertips to gradually bring in the flour, working in a circular motion.

Once you have a mostly combined mass, it's time to knead, either by hand or with a stand mixer. Knead well until the pasta dough becomes smooth, elastic and a little shiny. This can take between 7–10 minutes.

Once you are happy with your dough, wrap it in plastic wrap or a clean bag and rest it in the fridge for at least a few hours, but overnight is better.

While the dough is resting you can prepare the filling.

To make the filling, preheat the oven to 160°C (320°F).

Place the pumpkin into a bowl, pour over the ghee, sprinkle on the curry powder and use a spoon to combine. Place the pumpkin pieces on a baking tray, cover with foil and cook for about 20 minutes or until just softened. Remove the cover and cook the pumpkin for another 5 minutes to dry it out.

Mash or blend the pumpkin until it's smooth, then allow to cool.

Now, back to your dough. Make sure you bring it back to room temperature before you start rolling. Use a pasta machine and a rolling pin – you want nice large and long sheets of pasta dough rolled down to about 3 on a pasta machine.

To make your tortellini, cut the pasta into 6 cm (2½ in) squares. Use about 20 g (¾ oz) of filling per tortellini. Place the filling in the middle of each square and then, working on a piece at a time, hold the pasta square in your left hand with one of the points facing towards you. Use a finger on the other hand to lightly brush the top two edges with water, then fold the bottom corner to the top to form a triangle making sure there is no trapped air. Next, use the tips of your two pointer fingers to manoeuvre this filled bit up, while bringing in both edges in and around to seal; you are aiming to end up with little hat-like parcels (opposite).

Place the filled tortellini onto a lightly floured tray and refrigerate until you are ready to cook.

To serve, blanch the pasta and cook until ready; I like it a little past al dente. Serve in individual bowls with the kiri hodi warmed and poured over and topped with a spoon of sambol. Finish with a drizzle of olive oil.

Lamb mulligatawny

SERVES 6–8

When I was a child, my mum would talk about mulligatawny as a cure-all for when one was sick. The version she described sounded like a clear, brothy number, hot and fiery. And I do feel that at some stage my Nan fed me something that sounded like this, but on discussing, we became confused; maybe it was an oxtail soup that she used to do. Somewhere along the way things got muddled, and when I went hunting for recipes, they all told a different story. Turns out mulligatawny was one of those dishes that did start life as a Tamil soup but became something very different under British rule. And now I, too, shall mess with this recipe and present yet another version, which is a combination of confused memories, vague descriptions and my own opinions. This recipe makes lots, as all good soups should, as it's always handy to have extra to freeze or to drop around to your sick friends. As my mum said, it will fix what ails you.

- **130 g (4½ oz) Puy lentils**
- **9 g (⅓ oz) black peppercorns**
- **2 g (1⁄16 oz) coriander seeds**
- **½ cinnamon stick**
- **3 g (1⁄10 oz) salt flakes**
- **1½ g (1⁄32 oz) turmeric powder**
- **40 g (11½ oz) ghee**
- **11 g (⅓ oz) mustard seeds**
- **5 g (⅕ oz) picked curry leaves**
- **20 g (¾ oz) garlic, finely chopped**
- **30 g (1 oz) ginger, finely chopped**
- **200 g (7 oz) brown onion, finely diced**
- **100 g (3½ oz) (1 medium) carrot, cut into medium dice**
- **2–3 celery stalks, cut into medium dice (you should have equal amounts of carrot and celery)**
- **2 roma (plum) tomatoes, cut into medium dice**
- **200 ml (7 fl oz) coconut cream**
- **salt flakes**
- **juice of 1 lime**
- **1 bunch coriander (cilantro), washed and finely chopped, stalks and all (optional)**

To prepare the lamb, rinse your lamb pieces then place them in a saucepan with enough cold water to very generously cover. Slowly bring to a boil over a medium heat – this should be done slowly and take at least 30 minutes. As the water starts to simmer, take it off the heat, strain the meat and rinse in cold water. Set aside and clean your saucepan for the next step.

Return the saucepan to the stove and warm over a medium heat, then add a generous splash of oil. Once the oil is hot, add the onion and curry leaves and fry, stirring, for 2 minutes. Add in the spices and salt and continue cooking for another 2 minutes.

Add the lamb back in and cover with 2.4 litres (81 fl oz) of water; the liquid should be sitting a few centimetres over the meat. Bring this back up to a boil over a high heat, then turn it down and let it simmer gently for 2 hours. By this stage, the meat should be tender and the broth flavoursome. If you can, let everything sit in the liquid until cool and then refrigerate overnight before moving on to the next stage.

Once you are ready to make the soup, fish out your pieces of meat, keep and strain the broth, discarding any remaining solids.

Place the lentils in a saucepan, generously cover them with cold water and bring them to a boil. Strain and cool, then set aside.

LAMB
1 kg (2 lb 3 oz) lamb neck on the bone, cut into 3 cm (1¼ in) slices
good splash of neutral oil
300 g (10½ oz) brown onion, thickly sliced with the grain
3 g (⅒ oz) picked curry leaves
9 g (⅓ oz) coriander seeds
6 g (⅕ oz) cumin seeds
8 g (¼ oz) black peppercorns
6 cardamom pods, lightly crushed
3 cloves
5 g (⅕ oz) salt flakes

Combine the peppercorns, coriander seeds, cinnamon stick and salt, and finely grind in a small spice grinder or using a mortar and pestle. Stir in the turmeric powder.

In a large saucepan over a medium heat, add in your ghee and allow it to heat. Add the mustard seeds and curry leaves and stir, frying for about 10 seconds, until the leaves crisp.

Add in the garlic, ginger and onion and gently fry off, stirring so as not to colour, for another 3 minutes before adding in the spice mix for another minute of cooking – make sure to stir it or it will stick to the base. Add the carrot and celery and cook for another 2 minutes before adding the lentils. Give everything a good stir to combine, then add the reserved broth and the meat.

Bring this to a gentle simmer and let it cook for about 15 minutes. By this stage everything should be happy together, the lentils fully cooked and the meat warm and unctuous. Add in the tomato and the coconut cream and cook for a final 10–15 minutes. Have a taste for seasoning, maybe add a bit more salt and a little lime juice.

The flavour should be heavy with pepper and just a touch of sourness. Stir through the coriander just before serving in individual bowls.

Meatball curry

SERVES 4–6

I have a Sri Lankan cookbook – no names here – which I love for its sheer ridiculousness, as it veers wildly from tips on how to beautify your table with rose petals to traditional Lankan recipes to glamour photo shoots involving ballgowns, beaches and pizza. It's also where I first saw a reference to a meatball curry, so you will forgive me for thinking that this dish fell into the silly category (particularly because the dish was made using turkey meatballs). However, I have since come upon many more such references, and although I find the idea of meatballs and Sri Lanka in the same sentence confusing, it is actually a thing. And really, why not? Versions of meatballs appear in so many cultures. Perhaps we can even posit that they appeared on the island via the Dutch and their frikadels, which are one of the traditional components of lamprais. That is entirely guesswork on my part, but it kind of makes sense. Besides, I do love a meatball. I make this version using my staple Italian meatball-making method, and use a curry sauce instead of a tomatoey one. And so, here is my meatball curry, something I first snickered at but now love. It just goes to show, one mustn't be too hasty to judge. This can be eaten with rice, as part of a larger banquet, or put it with pasta and make spaghetti and meatballs. Any leftovers can be used to make a meatball sandwich or a bánh mì (page 92).

SAUCE

- 100 g (3½ oz) ghee
- 10 g (⅓ oz) picked curry leaves
- 5 g (⅕ oz) mustard seeds
- 350 g (12½ oz) brown onions, diced
- 35 g (1¼ oz) finely chopped garlic
- 30 g (1 oz) finely chopped ginger
- 2 long red chillies, cut into thin rounds
- 15 g (½ oz) Brown curry powder (page 27)
- 3 cardamom pods, bruised
- 1 rampe (pandan) leaf, tied
- 330 g (11½ oz) tinned chopped tomatoes
- 300 ml (10 fl oz) coconut cream
- salt flakes and freshly ground black pepper

To make the sauce, warm a large, wide-based saucepan over a medium heat and then add in the ghee. Once warmed, add the curry leaves and mustard seeds, fry a little to temper and then add the onion, garlic, ginger and chilli. Cook, stirring occasionally for about 5 minutes, until the onions are softened. You don't want to get any colour here. Season well.

Add the curry powder and continue cooking and stirring for 1 minute. The curry powder will start to stick to the base.

Add in the cardamom, rampe (pandan), tomato and coconut along with 300 ml (10 fl oz) water and bring to a simmer. Simmer the sauce gently for about 30 minutes, then set aside.

For the meatballs, place the garlic, ginger, curry leaves, turmeric, coriander roots and stems in a blender and blitz to form a paste. Set aside.

In a large mixing bowl, throw the pork and beef together and around, slapping and working the mixture until it starts to emulsify and becomes sticky. Add in the paste and the remaining dry ingredients and continue mixing until you have a thoroughly homogenised, emulsified mix. This step can be done in a stand mixer.

MEATBALLS

- 20 g (¾ oz) garlic cloves
- 15 g (½ oz) ginger
- 15 g (½ oz) picked curry leaves
- 8 g (¼ oz) fresh turmeric
- 1 bunch coriander (cilantro), roots and stems washed, leaves picked and roughly chopped, to garnish
- 500 g (1 lb 2 oz) coarsely minced (ground) fatty pork
- 500 g (1 lb 2 oz) finely minced (ground) beef
- 15 g (½ oz) chilli flakes
- 10 g (¼ oz) ground Maldive fish flakes
- 5 g (⅕ oz) roasted and ground fenugreek
- 5 g (⅕ oz) cooking salt
- 5 g (⅕ oz) ground black pepper
- olive oil, to drizzle

Preheat the oven to 200°C (390°F).

Lightly oil a large baking tray and then use your hands to form meatballs weighing 40 g (1½ oz) each. As you roll them, place them directly onto the tray, leaving a nice amount of space between each one (you may need two trays). You should end up with about 30 meatballs. Drizzle with a little oil.

Place the meatballs in the oven for 15 minutes, then remove from the oven and gently place the meatballs in the saucepan with the sauce.

Simmer everything together over a low heat for 30 minutes.

Serve hot, garnished with the chopped coriander leaves.

Kangaroo tail curry

SERVES 4

If there was one curry from this book that I would love to be embraced by the world, this would be it. Although it makes sense for us to eat more of it in Australia, there is a still a weird cultural barrier that's kept kangaroo from pushing into the mainstream. You can buy it in most supermarkets now, but only in small amounts and only particular cuts. My favourite cut, the tail, which is used here, is a little trickier to come by. But it is the most glorious part of the animal, and works in much the same way as oxtail does. It needs to be cooked low and slow to reveal unctuous fatty and flavourful morsels of meat that fall from the bone. This is best done in some sort of braise, so we adapted the flavours of our dry black curry to make it saucy, and added extra black pepper for kick and jaggery for a sweet stickiness. If you're not in Australia, substitute with oxtail but if you are here, please try and find some kangaroo or even wallaby tail to make this because it is both delicious and good for our land. This is a particularly strongly flavoured fiery curry.

- 1.2 kg (2 lb 10 oz) kangaroo tail, cut into 6 cm (2½ in) rounds
- 40 g (1½ oz) ghee
- 5 g (⅕ oz) picked curry leaves
- 600 g (1 lb 5 oz) red onion, finely sliced
- 20 g (¾ oz) finely chopped garlic
- 15 g (½ oz) finely chopped ginger
- 15 g (½ oz) lemongrass stem, white part only, finely chopped
- 2 long red chillies, finely chopped
- 30 g (1 oz) Black curry powder (page 29)
- 20 g (¾ oz) chilli powder
- 6 g (⅕ oz) cardamom seeds
- 260 g (9 oz) jaggery, chopped
- 14 g (½ oz) tamarind concentrate or paste
- salt flakes and freshly ground black pepper
- juice of 1–2 limes

First wash in cold water and then place your tail pieces in a large saucepan and fill with double the amount of cold water. Place over a medium heat and bring to a boil. Once boiled, strain the tail pieces, give them a rinse in cold water and set aside.

Place a wide-based saucepan, big enough to hold all of the tail, over a medium heat, add in the ghee and allow to heat. Once hot, add in the curry leaves and fry, cooking for a moment or so before adding in the red onion, garlic, ginger, lemongrass and chilli. Season gently. Cook, stirring occasionally, for 7–8 minutes, until the onions have softened.

Add in the curry and chilli powders and the cardamom seeds, then cook for 4–5 minutes, until the chilli powder darkens considerably. You will need to stir continuously as you cook, trying not to breathe in too much of the spice.

Add in the jaggery and continue stirring for 2–3 minutes, until it has all melted and begun to caramelise.

Return the tail pieces to the pan along with 1.4 litres (47 fl oz) of water and the tamarind. Bring your curry up to a boil, then reduce to a simmer and continue cooking for about 2 hours, until the kangaroo pieces are unctuous and the meat is starting to give way.

Taste for seasoning – it should be black pepper-heavy. Add the fresh lime juice just before you are ready to serve.

Black spiced beef brisket

SERVES 6–8

I love when you think you have a grasp on a particular food culture and then along comes a recipe completely unlike anything you've previously seen. And the beauty of it is, the more you look the more this will happen, and continue to happen. It still does to me – every time I visit Sri Lanka I taste at least one new dish that is a revelation. (The latest being a mushroom sambol that was super hot and excellent, but sadly didn't make it into this book.) One time, that dish was when my Nan showed me how to make beef smore, a Burgher dish that came from the European idea of a pot roast – basically meat with gravy, but this gravy was made with curry powder and lime pickle. When I started making it, the whole pot roasting thing didn't make sense so I went for a slow-cooked version. There is great ease to this method; once it's in you don't have to do very much. The flavours of the smore somehow then morphed into using more of the traditional ingredients of a black spiced curry. So in actual fact, this is nothing like the smore that I first had an epiphany with, but it has ended up as this dish, which is very worthy of making. Do this as the centrepiece for a curry banquet or roast Sunday lunch and, if there are leftovers, these will be very good in a roti (page 100) or a sandwich (page 95).

- 1.8 kg (4 lb) piece beef brisket, at room temperature
- salt flakes
- 100 g (3½ oz) Black curry powder (page 29)
- 50 g (1¾ oz) ghee
- 240 g (8½ oz) eschalots, thinly sliced
- 12 g (½ oz) garlic cloves, coarsely chopped
- 10 g (⅓ oz) ginger, coarsely chopped
- 10 g (⅓ oz) lemongrass, white part only, coarsely chopped
- 15 g (½ oz) picked curry leaves
- 2 long red chillies, cut into thin rounds
- 120 g (4½ oz) tamarind pulp, rehydrated in water and then sieved to separate the seeds
- Potato galette (page 209), to serve
- Brussels sprouts with mustard (page 203), to serve

Season the brisket with salt, then rub with half the black curry powder. Heat a frying pan large enough to hold the meat over a high heat, then add the ghee. Give it a moment to heat up, then slip in the brisket. Let it sit for 2–3 minutes before turning and searing the other side for another 2–3 minutes, until browned. Transfer to a deep baking dish that holds the brisket snugly.

Preheat the oven to 150°C (300°F).

Add the eschalot, garlic, ginger, lemongrass, curry leaves and chilli to the pan you used to sear the brisket. Stir over a high heat for a few minutes, then add the remaining black curry powder. Stir well, as the spices will stick to the pan, and cook for about 4 minutes. Add the tamarind and 500 ml (17 fl oz) of water. Stir and bring to a boil, then pour the mixture over the brisket. Cover the brisket with a sheet of baking paper, then foil, and cook in the oven for 5–6 hours, until gelatinous. Rest in the pan for 20–30 minutes.

Thickly slice the brisket and serve with the cooking juices poured over. (You may want to skim some of the fat off the top first, but I like to keep it.)

Serve with potato galette and brussels sprouts with mustard.

Buryani

SERVES 8
PEOPLE

Buryani, or biryani as the whole world knows it except in Sri Lanka, where they like to spell things a bit differently, is a classic dish with versions found far and wide. Whether it originated in India or Pakistan is up for debate but, at its basis, it is a dish of layered rice, usually with a meat curry (although fried chicken is a popular modern version, and one found a lot in Sri Lanka). Sometimes the rice is par-cooked first, sometimes the whole thing is cooked together.

Traditionally it's a celebratory dish, and often a large platter of it is served for everyone to share. In Sri Lanka it is usually made with chicken, which is why I never really paid much attention to it. That was until I wrote LF, and suddenly I decided we needed a buryani recipe. So I did some research and came up with a version to put in the book, aware of the irony that until then, it was something I'd ignored. Not long after the book came out we wanted to offer a weekly special that would only be available on one night, something to entice people at the start of our week. And so I decided we would do a buryani night. We would do a different version each week, cooked and then layered in a chatty pot and served with a sambol and some other little sides. And so we did, coming up with new versions each week – seafood ones, vegetarian ones and all sorts of meat ones. A little while later, we decided to open on Monday nights. We launched this extra night with a guest chef series, so for the first sixteen Mondays I coerced various chef friends into doing their own version.

It was an excellent series, with some chefs trying their hand at traditional Indian and Lankan flavours, while others stayed closer to their chosen cuisine, and others became very much a collaboration. One of these was a Cuban–Lankan combination, which was surprisingly seamless. We had all sorts of chefs, all sorts of ways. Chazzy even did one. The kitchen staff loved it, as we got to experiment and play and work with other clever chefs. There were too many different menus to speak of here, and too many recipes around this theme, but the very first was one of the finest, cooked by Muu (he was the guinea pig). Here is his buryani menu:

WHITE PEPPER BRISKET & BONE MARROW
ONION & CURRY LEAF TEMPERED SAMBA RICE
HERB, ONION & CUCUMBER SALAD
SESAME SAMBOL
GODAMBA ROTI

This is a recipe that needs to be prepared over at least 2 days. The bone marrow needs to soak overnight and the brisket needs a first cooking and then a second. If you serve it in the dish you cook it in – you will need a large baking dish or clay pot. To make it a true celebration, see my suggestions overleaf for what to serve with it.

8 pieces bone marrow, cut into 8 cm (3¼ in) pieces and split down the middle

cooking salt

100 g (3½ oz) ghee

coriander (cilantro) leaves, picked, reserving half of the leaves, to garnish

Cabbage, onion, sesame and Maldive fish (page 200), to serve

Moru chilli sambol (page 37), to serve

Pistachio, almond, cardamom and kithul raita (page 46), to serve

Dhal (page 212)

pappadums or toasted Kade paan (page 106) are also good additions

BEEF

75 g (2¾ oz) garlic cloves

320 g (11½ oz) peeled Thai eschalots

10 coriander stalks, roots attached, roots washed, half leaves picked, all the stems kept

5½ g (⅕ oz) salt flakes

30 g (1 oz) white peppercorns, roasted and coarsely ground

20 g (¾ oz) coriander seeds, roasted and coarsely ground

2 kg (4 lb 6 oz) beef brisket, at room temperature, cut into 10 cm (4 in) square chunks

oil for browning

50 ml (1¾ fl oz) vegetable oil

100 ml (3½ fl oz) arrack

160 g (5½ oz) jaggery, grated or chopped

160 ml (5½ fl oz) fish sauce

200 ml (7 fl oz) peanut oil

750 ml (25½ fl oz) coconut milk

The day before you are going to serve the dish, prepare your bone marrow. Combine water and salt (5 per cent salt to water) to make a cold-water brine, enough to generously cover the bone marrow. Let the marrow sit at least overnight in the brine in your fridge.

For the beef, use a mortar and pestle to pound together the garlic, shallots, coriander roots and salt flakes until the mixture forms a paste. Mix through the ground white pepper and coriander seeds, then set aside.

In a large frying pan heat the oil over a high heat, brown the brisket in batches, transferring to a large baking dish as you go.

Once all the meat is browned, add the vegetable oil and half the ground paste to the same pan (keep the other half aside in the fridge for stage two) and fry this off over a medium heat, stirring continuously until it becomes a dark brown. Add the arrack and reduce it until it's evaporated, then add in half of the jaggery. Cook until the mixture is deeply caramelised and dark to the edge, then add the fish sauce, stir and let it cook for a further 2 minutes. Add this to the dish with the brisket, scraping the bottom of the pan to remove all of the solids.

Preheat the oven to 150°C (300°F).

Cover the meat with 2 litres (68 fl oz) of water and bring to a boil. The water should cover the meat; if not, add a little more. Once it's boiling, cover with baking paper and then a lid or foil and cook in the oven for about 3 hours, until the brisket is tender but not falling apart. Let the brisket cool completely in the liquid before removing from the liquid and placing in the fridge. Refrigerate until completely cold and dried out a little. Reserve the liquid to cook your rice, though you may not need it all.

Once the meat is cold, cut each piece into quarters. Place a wok over high heat, add the peanut oil and heat until shimmering. Add the reserved paste and fry until golden brown. Add the cold pieces of meat and then the remaining jaggery, stirring. Once caramelised, add in the fish sauce and stir.

Add the coconut milk, all the coriander stems and half the leaves and bring to a simmer. Taste for seasoning. Cook this all together until the liquid is almost completely gone and the meat is very gelatinous. Remove from the stove and use tongs or a fork to pull the meat apart into curry-sized pieces. Set aside.

Cook your rice in a rice cooker using the reserved braising liquid. Lean on the side of only just enough liquid as you really don't want soggy rice here. While the rice is cooking, make your temper.

Heat the ghee in a frying pan over a high heat. Once it's shimmering, add in the curry leaves and mustard seeds. Give them a moment to fry, then add the onion. Cook this mix over a high heat, stirring often, until the onion starts to darken and become caramelised. Season well and set aside.

Combine your rice and temper mix, then season to taste with salt and white pepper. A couple of hours before you are ready to serve, bring the bone marrow to room temperature and lay it out, split side up, on a baking tray.

To bring it all together, first preheat the oven to 180°C (360°F).

Place a large baking dish or clay pot on your stove, heat well and then add the ghee. Once the ghee is shimmering, spoon in half your tempered rice and flatten it down so it covers the base in a single layer. Spoon in the brisket – again, you want this in an even layer – and then finish with the remaining rice. Cover your dish with foil or a lid and let it

RICE

600 g (1 lb 5 oz) koshihkari rice

salt flakes and ground white pepper

TEMPER

60 g (2 oz) ghee

5 g (1/5 oz) picked curry leaves

4 g (1/8 oz) mustard seeds

300 g (10½ oz) brown onion, diced

salt flakes and ground white pepper

sit over a high heat for about 10 minutes. You want time for the rice to crisp but not burn. If you listen carefully it should start crackling a little – this means it's nearly ready. Transfer to the oven and cook for a further 20 minutes until everything is hot through. The time can vary depending on the warmth of your ingredients as you constructed them.

Meanwhile, slip your bone marrow into the same oven and cook for 10 minutes. Remove from the oven and let it sit somewhere warm while the buryani cooks.

Serve the buryani hot from the oven garnished with the remaining coriander leaves. Serve the bone marrow on the side, encourage guests to scrape it onto their rice and mix it through, along with the accompaniments suggested in the recipe list or any others to your liking.

Duck padre curry

MAKES 1 DUCK'S WORTH

This is a dish that I read about in Charmaine Solomon's very excellent *Complete Asian Cookbook*. It intrigued me, as I don't think I've ever eaten duck in Sri Lanka and you rarely see Lankan recipes that use alcohol. The story goes that as priests weren't allowed to drink booze, this was the dish that won them over, as it was the only way they could get some alcohol into them. Most versions I have found of this recipe are fairly rustic, but what I have for you here is our restaurant version – this just means it's more complicated to do, and looks fancier on the plate. I have given quantities for one duck, but there are various ways you can utilise this dish. The legs and breast are cooked separately, the legs cooked in the sauce as you would normally with a curry and the breasts simply pan-fried and served with the sauce. This means you have options, depending on how you want to serve it and how many people you are feeding. This is a very restauranty way of going about things – often everything is prepared and cooked, and then you can finish the final cooking later in whichever way you want. I have suggested the best way of dealing with all of the cuts. You can use them all at once, and you will have a very fine and super fancy curry meal fit for many people, or you can do it in parts and just eat the breasts, keeping the legs to be eaten later or shredded, the meat used to make a pan roll or fill a patty. Hopefully once you read the recipe, this will all make a lot more sense.

- 1 whole duck
- 5 g (⅕ oz) picked curry leaves
- 200 g (7 oz) diced brown onion
- 17 g (⅔ oz) garlic cloves, chopped
- 15 g (½ oz) ginger, chopped
- 10 g (⅓ oz) long red chilli, sliced into rounds
- 10 g (⅓ oz) Brown curry powder (page 27)
- ½ cinnamon stick
- 1 piece star anise
- 1 rampe (pandan) leaf, tied
- 1 lemongrass stem, white part only, bruised
- 300 ml (10 fl oz) coconut cream
- salt flakes

SAUCE

- 100 ml (3½ fl oz) arrack
- 100 g (3½ oz) jaggery, grated or chopped
- 25–35 ml (1–1¼ oz) cider vinegar

The first step is to break down the duck into specific cuts – you'll need a sharp knife and a cleaver for this bit. You want to end up with the breasts (these can be kept in the fridge until later), the legs, the wing in three pieces (the tip, the middle and the larger bit that connects to the breast) and the rest of the carcass cut into large chunks. Reserve any bits of duck fat and stray skin to render and use for later.

If what I have just written makes no sense to you, you have three options: learn a bit about animal butchery, find a butcher to do it for you, or buy whatever bits you want to use and adapt this recipe to suit.

Preheat the oven to 150°C (300°F).

Find a large roasting dish, big enough to hold the duck, and warm it on your stovetop over a medium heat. Splash in some oil and then add the duck carcass and the tip of the wing, keeping aside the breasts (they should be in the fridge), the legs and the other two bits of the wing.

Brown the carcass over the stove, turning as you go, until the bones become a dark golden brown. There should be enough fat still lurking that you don't need any extra oil for this.

Add all the remaining ingredients apart from the liquids, season and give it all for a couple of minutes to cook. Add in the coconut cream and 450 ml (15 fl oz) of water and bring to a simmer. Once simmering, slip in the legs and wing bits and add more water if needed to cover. Place a sheet of baking paper over the top, then cover with a lid or foil and braise the duck in the oven for 1 hour, until the legs are cooked through.

Remove from the oven and allow to cool completely.

Once cooled, fish out your duck legs (unless something's weird you will have two) and wing bits (you should have four pieces) and set aside. Strain the liquid through a fine strainer into a saucepan.

To make the sauce, add the arrack and jaggery to the strained cooking liquid and reduce by half. You should have a thick, luxurious sauce, sticky and rich. Season with cider vinegar and salt, if you think it needs it.

Once you are ready to serve, this is how you deal with the various bits depending on what you have decided to do.

WING BITS

Have them heating in the sauce, if you haven't already eaten them as a snack, and serve them alongside the legs and/or breast. (If you want to be really fancy, deep fry them first before sitting them in the sauce.)

LEGS

Preheat the oven to 180°C (360°F). Place some of the rendered duck fat you made earlier in a frying pan and get it nice and hot, then gently add in the legs, skin-side down, and brown them over a medium–high heat for a few minutes. Place in the oven for about 10 minutes and, once hot, serve skin-side up with a puddle of sauce.

BREASTS

Season your duck breasts heavily and then place them, skin-side down, in a cold, heavy-based frying pan. Sit the pan over a medium–high heat for about 1 minute, until you hear the duck skin start to sizzle and see some of the fat rendering. Turn the heat to low and slowly cook the duck for another 9–10 minutes, pouring out any excess fat into a bowl along the way (you will use this again). By this stage the duck skin should be a lovely deep brown.

Flip the duck and cook for another 2–3 minutes before removing it from the pan and letting it sit somewhere warm to rest. Cut into slices to serve, and pour over the sauce.

FAT

Place all your duck scraps into a small saucepan and cover with cold water. Place this over a gentle heat and keep cooking until the water has evaporated and the fat has separated out. Strain through a fine strainer. This fat will last for ages in your fridge and is very good to cook with, especially roasting potatoes which would be a good accompaniment for this dish.

OTHER

THINGS

SALADS, THE BEAUTY OF KIRI HODI AND DHAL

The bits on the side are often the best. These are all the extra things, the excellent companions, there to enhance the main event. Often, these sorts of dishes are vegetable-based, and without them, the symphony of a meal would collapse.

This little section is here to celebrate these sides. We have some salads, even though they're not really a traditional Sri Lankan thing. Over there, what we think of as salads fall into two categories. You can have something like, say, a cucumber sambol, which to the unsuspecting Western eye looks like a crisp cooling accompaniment, but is actually laden with green chilli and is hotter than anything else on the table. Or there are mallungs, which are like a salad in theory. The term is used to describe an array of quick-cooked dishes, often leafy greens, but can also cover anything from leeks to green papaya.

Here, too, we embrace kiri hodi, milk gravy, a Sri Lankan classic which is like a starter curry sauce. It's runny and saucy, usually mild, sweet with coconut and only slightly spiced. It's delicious enough to eat on its own with a bowl of rice or some string hoppers, and is also a perfect sauce, subtle enough to readily adapt into all sorts of Western dishes, adding just an accent of Sri Lanka.

And there's my dhal too, straight up, not to be messed with.

If you are interested in making a Sri Lankan style rice and curry banquet using recipes from this book, then take a few things from here – dhal, of course, is one of the essentials – to go with a curry from the Generously Sized Things chapter and add a sambol or two. Or, if you are planning a more European style meal, one of these with, say, the tortellini (page 172) would be most satisfactory. Some of these recipes also work on their own as an easy lunch or dinner. Or maybe you are having a barbecue or picnic and need some extra salad ideas. There is a little bit of something for everyone here, to provide the much-needed balance we all search for.

Pineapple, cucumber, red onion and tomato

SERVES 4–6

This is my version of a salad I ate at a restaurant called Beach Wadiya in Colombo. The restaurant sits on the edge of the ocean and the tables are all set up on the sand. I have a slight aversion to sand, especially near food, but somehow I find it acceptable here. The restaurant has been there forever, and last time I mentioned how I loved it it to a Colombo socialite they were slightly shocked and said it was a very retro choice. It has a dilapidated charm, and they do an excellent kang kung with garlic and a good crab curry, which is all I really need. Last time I was there I discovered a new thing, this salad, and immediately knew it was one to steal. I forgot to take a photo before devouring it, so all I have is my taste memory and a blurry shot of some stray onion slices and a puddle of leftover juice. This is a very simple salad, so it relies on having the best ingredients – you will need nice sweet pineapples and proper tomatoes. The cutting of the ingredients also becomes very important. You want the pineapple, cucumber and tomato to all be roughly the same size. It feels better in your mouth somehow.

- 200 g (7 oz) cucumber
- 200 g (7 oz) tomato
- 100 g (3½ oz) red onion
- 250 g (9 oz) peeled pineapple
- 2 long green chillies
- lime juice
- salt flakes and freshly ground black pepper
- a small splash of extra virgin olive oil

To prepare the cucumber, peel the skin, cut the cucumbers in half lengthways and scrape out the seeds. Cut again in half lengthways, then cut across in 2 cm (¾ in) pieces to form quarter moons. Place in a small mixing bowl, season with a pinch of sea salt, mix and set aside.

Cut the tomato into a 2 cm (¾ in) dice and place in a small mixing bowl. Season with a pinch of sea salt, mix and set aside.

Cut the red onion into 5 mm (¼ in) slices with the grain and place in a small mixing bowl. Season with a pinch of sea salt, massage this into the onion well and set aside.

Cut the pineapple into a 2 cm (¾ in) dice and set aside in a larger mixing bowl.

Cut your green chillies in half lengthways, scrape out the seeds, then finely slice the chilli on a slight diagonal into thin strips. Add these to the bowl with the pineapple.

Once your salted ingredients have sat for at least 30 minutes, add them to the bowl with the pineapple. Strain any excess liquid from the cucumbers and squeeze the onions, but the tomatoes can go straight in, juice and all.

Mix well and season with an excessive amount of black pepper, enough lime juice to make the salad sharp and just a splash of olive oil.

Watermelon, black olive, tomato and katta sambol

SERVES 4

There are some dishes or combinations that are somehow just perfect. The first time I did a version of this salad was at Berta, and just three simple ingredients – tomato, watermelon and black olive – made a little bit of magic. When those moments happen in cooking land you hold onto to them, bringing them with you wherever you go, prodding them and adapting them to suit the circumstances you find yourself in. And so I have turned my Italian Lankan and created a new version of this salad. The simplicity is the same, the balance of sweet, salty and acidic, with a new addition of chilli heat. It is very refreshing and fits nicely with many of the dishes found in this book.

- 120 g (4½ oz) kalamata olives
- 300 g (10½ oz) cherry tomatoes
- 50 g (1¾ oz) Katta sambol (page 34)
- approximately 800 g (1 lb 12 oz) watermelon
- 5 g (⅕ oz) picked curry leaves, fried
- a healthy splash of extra virgin olive oil

Preheat the oven to 100°C (210°F).

Pit the kalamata olives and tear them in half lengthways. Place them on a baking tray lined with baking paper and dry them in the oven for 3 hours. Remove and set aside to cool.

Cut the cherry tomatoes in half and place them in a mixing bowl with the katta sambol. Stir to combine, then set aside to sit for an hour.

Ball your watermelon using a small Parisian scoop. You want to end up with balls a similar size to the tomatoes, and in equal amounts. Reserve any juices and eat the leftover bits of watermelon.

To serve, add the watermelon balls, reserved juices and the olives to the tomato and katta mix. Add the olive oil, mix well and serve laid out in a large shallow bowl. Garnish with the fried curry leaves and serve immediately.

Cabbage, onion, sesame and Maldive fish

SERVES 4

If you know me at all then you've probably heard me say this before, but I do love a cabbage salad. Cabbages are a very fine brassica, sturdy with an excellent texture and usually fairly cheap. They last for a long time and they're a great flavour carrier without giving up their own identity, which, depending on the variety, can be sharp, mustardy, juicy or slightly sweet. Cabbage is a perfect side with so many things as it's refreshing and crunchy and offers relief when things are getting a bit rich, or texturally too soft. I have made so many versions of a cabbage salad, but this one was inspired by the fresh cabbage you get in Japan when eating a pork katsu. And then while thinking about Japan, it struck me how similar katsuobushi is to Maldive fish, so in that went, and then I was thinking about gomashio, so the salad got toasted sesame seeds too.

- 4 g (⅛ oz) Maldive fish flakes
- 2 g (1⁄16 oz) white peppercorns
- 30 g (1 oz) white sesame seeds, toasted
- 2 g (1⁄16 oz) Fermented chilli powder (page 63) (optional)
- 100 g (3½ oz) eschalots
- 10 g (⅓ oz) cooking salt
- ½ small white cabbage (approximately 500 g/1 lb 2 oz)
- 1 g (1⁄32 oz) salt flakes
- juice of 1 lime
- small splash of extra virgin olive oil
- salt flakes and freshly ground black pepper

Using a mortar and pestle, pound the Maldive fish flakes and peppercorns with a pinch of salt until finely ground. Add in the toasted sesame seeds and pound just enough to break them down a little, stir through the fermented chilli powder and then set aside.

Thinly slice your eschalots into ½ mm (1⁄64 in) rounds using a mandolin. Mix the cooking salt with 500 ml (17 fl oz) water, add the eschalot slices and soak in the fridge for between 30 minutes and 2 hours.

Shave the cabbage on a mandolin as finely as you can. Place it in a bowl and mix through the salt flakes, massaging it into the cabbage. Let this sit for 10 minutes before squeezing it dry and placing it into a fresh mixing bowl.

Drain the eschalot, use your hands to gently squeeze it dry and then add to the cabbage. Add the lime juice, olive oil, a good amount of black pepper and the sesame mix and combine well. Taste for seasoning and then serve immediately.

Sprinkle the top with extra fermented chilli powder, if you have it.

Brussels sprouts

Here's an underrated brassica, a vegetable with a bad reputation that probably came about because people historically insisted on overboiling them, serving them soft and stinky. Poor Brussels (on a side note, I always find the s on the end of their name slightly strange). But let me extol their virtues. They are mustardy and sharp in the same way as cabbage, and work wonderfully as a salad when raw and shaved. They are also very happy when charry and smoky, they are small and green and cute, and a branch of growing brussels is a Dr Seuss delight to look at. I think we all need more of them in our life.

Fried with mustard

SERVES 4 AS PART OF A MEAL

This dish is leaning towards the darker side, giving deep charred bits and maintaining a firm bite on the inside – no softness here. The flavour too, is strong and sharp – mustard for spice tempered a little with the buttery notes of ghee. This would be a very good side dish served with roast chicken and potato galette (page 209), an easy way to Lankify a Sunday roast.

- 600 g (1lb 5 oz) brussels sprouts
- vegetable oil, for deep-frying
- 30 g (1 oz) ghee, melted
- 20 g (¾ oz) Mustard (page 44)
- juice of 1–2 limes
- salt flakes and freshly ground black pepper

Cut your brussels sprouts in half from top to bottom, then use your fingers to ruffle and loosen their leaves a little so they look slightly dishevelled.

Add vegetable oil to a depth of about 3 cm (1¼ in) in a large saucepan, then heat the oil to 180°C (360°F). Deep-fry the sprouts in batches, for about 3 minutes per batch. You want the outer leaves to start looking burnt, but still with a firmness to their insides. Set aside to drain on a wire rack.

In a large mixing bowl, add the ghee, mustard and good squeeze of lime juice and mix to combine. Add in the brussels, season well and toss them to coat.

Serve immediately.

Mallung

SERVES 2–4 AS PART OF A MEAL

This dish is in the style of a Lankan mallung, a side dish that is kind of salad like and only just cooked. You get the crisp texture of the sprouts, and their sharp flavour stands up to the Maldive fish and is balanced with the gentleness of the fresh coconut. And there's a little spice and chilli to liven it all up. This is an excellent side dish, but add a poached egg or two on top and you have an easy little lunch.

- 30 g (1 oz) ghee
- 4 g (⅛ oz) mustard seeds
- 6 g (⅕ oz) Maldive fish flakes
- 2 green bird's-eye chillies, finely sliced
- 6 g (⅕ oz) picked curry leaves
- 280 g (10 oz) brussels sprouts, finely shaved lengthways on a mandolin
- 3 g (⅒ oz) turmeric powder
- 50 g (1¾ oz) grated coconut
- juice of ½–1 lime
- salt flakes and freshly ground black pepper

Warm a wide-based frying pan over a high heat, then add in the ghee, mustard seeds, Maldive fish flakes, chilli and curry leaves.

Cook, stirring, until the mustard seeds start to pop and the curry leaves fry. Add the brussels sprouts and give everything a good mix. Season heavily with salt and pepper and continue stirring.

After a few minutes, sprinkle over the turmeric, stir to combine and then add in the coconut.

Continue cooking and stirring for 2–3 minutes, until the sprouts are just starting to give way yet still hold a little crunch. Remove from the heat, add the lime juice and check your seasoning. You want to taste the black pepper quite strongly and you also want a sharp kick from the lime.

Lay out on a shallow dish to serve.

Kiri hodi

This next little section is a great example of what I have been speaking about throughout this whole book – the virtues of having a great staple sauce or thing, and then finding multiple ways to use it. Slight variations and tweaks will give you any number of new dishes. Kiri hodi is very simple. It translates to milk (kiri) gravy (hodi) and is made with a base including onions and fenugreek and lots of coconut milk. It's always very saucy, often quite mild, and comes in variations – it can be made with added tomato or potato or boiled eggs or Maldive fish, to name but a few. It's served as an accompaniment to string hoppers, hoppers, pittu, kottu roti and rice, and is a comfort food for when you are sick, or a gentle starter for small people before they move on to hotter curries. It is mildly spiced with just a hint of curry powder and slightly sweet from the coconut milk. It is complex enough to be slurped tastily on its own, but can also adapt itself to any number of dishes, flavours and extra ingredients. Could it be Sri Lanka's answer to chicken stock? A bold statement to be sure, but one that gets a head wobble from me. A side note: some bits of fish, gently simmered in this gravy, became my son Lenny's go-to dinner when he ate at LFS, thus proving its adaptability and appropriateness for young people.

Kiri hodi

SERVES 6–8

The name translates to 'milk gravy', which is exactly what this is: a gentle dish that is more like a sauce than a curry. Kiri hodi is a great starter curry for kids or those in need of comfort. You can pop almost anything into it. I love it most served as an accompaniment to string hoppers, where its excellent sauciness soaks into the delicate strands.

- 5 g (⅕ oz) fenugreek seeds
- 25 g (1 oz) coconut oil
- 4 g (⅛ oz) picked curry leaves, finely sliced along the grain
- 150 g (5½ oz) sliced brown onion
- 12 g (½ oz) finely chopped garlic
- 8 g (¼ oz) White curry powder (page 26)
- 3 g (⅒ oz) turmeric powder
- 1 cinnamon stick
- 250 ml (8½ fl oz) coconut cream
- 4 × 5 cm (2 in) pieces rampe (pandan) leaf
- juice of up to 1 lime
- salt flakes and freshly ground white pepper

Place the fenugreek seeds in a small bowl, add 75 ml (2½ fl oz) of water and set aside.

Melt the coconut oil in a medium saucepan over a medium heat, add the curry leaves and cook, stirring for a minute or so, until the leaves are fried. Add the onion and garlic and cook, stirring occasionally, for 4–5 minutes, until the onion has softened.

Stir in the curry powder, turmeric and cinnamon and continue stirring for 1–2 minutes until the powder begins to catch on the bottom of the pan.

Add the coconut cream, rampe (pandan) leaf, soaked fenugreek seeds and 600 ml (20½ fl oz) of water. Bring the mixture just to a boil, then reduce the heat and simmer gently for 2–3 minutes, until the sauce comes together. Season to taste with lime juice, salt and pepper. The flavour should be mild and sweet with just a hint of curry and pepper, and lime in the very background.

With charred cabbage and chilli crunch

SERVES 2–4

This is a very excellent side dish and, may I say, quite fashionable, as a hunk of charred cabbage is all the rage at the moment, and rightly so. Cooking it this way gives a smoky bitterness to the vegetable to balance its sweetness, and texturally it's a delight too. The brief cook gives you char and slightly softens the cabbage, cooking it just enough to maintain its texture and body while also letting it relax a little. The kiri hodi tempers the charred bits and adds sauciness to the soft.

- 1 whole hispi cabbage, approximately 400 g (14 oz)
- 30 g (1 oz) ghee, liquified
- salt flakes and freshly ground black pepper
- 200 g (7 oz) Kiri hodi (page 205), hot
- Lankan chilli crunch (page 39), to serve

Cut your cabbage into quarters from the root to the top. Rub the outside with ghee and season with a little salt and black pepper.

Warm a heavy-based frying pan over a high heat, then add your cabbage pieces cut-side down. Turn the heat to medium and let the cabbage sit for about 3 minutes, until it blackens. Repeat on the other cut side, and also on the curved edge.

Transfer the cabbage straight onto a plate and arrange prettily with the curved outside bit sitting down on the plate. Pour over the kiri hodi and spoon on some chilli crunch and serve immediately.

Potato galette

SERVES 4

This is a labour-intensive dish; it's not technically tricky, but does take a little time to build. It is, however, fantastical looking (and tasting), and a very good dinner party dish as it can be made and cooked the day before to be easily finished when you are ready. Potatoes traditionally go in kiri hodi anyway; we're just fluffing them up, cooking them in a slightly fancier, more restaurant-style way. The beauty of this is you get excellent textures. The potatoes sticking out at the top are roasty and crisp, then when you dig in you get the soft silkiness of a braised potato. And because of its only very gentle spiced flavour, this dish works equally as well in a Sri Lankan meal as it would alongside, say, a roast dinner or a simple steak, or anywhere you need a good potato side dish. And one always needs a good potato on the side if you ask me.

- 120 g (4½ oz) ghee
- 2 kg (4 lb 6 oz) Dutch cream potatoes, washed, skins on
- 5 g (⅕ oz) salt flakes
- 5 g (⅕ oz) black pepper
- 500 ml (17 fl oz) Kiri hodi (page 205)

Melt your ghee until it liquifies, then pour it into a large mixing bowl. Using a mandolin, slice your potatoes to 1 mm (1⁄32 in) thick. Place them into the bowl with the ghee, coating as you go.

Once the potatoes are all sliced and coated, season with the salt and pepper and give them a good mix.

Strain your kiri hodi through a fine strainer. Reserve the liquid, then gather all the bits from the strainer and spread them along the base of your baking dish.

Preheat the oven to 150°C (300°F).

Now you can start arranging the potatoes. Stack a pile in your hands as you would for cards and sit them upright in your dish, starting on an edge. You can do them in straight lines or curve them around, as you can see opposite.

Pour the reserved kiri hodi liquid over the potatoes. Lay a sheet of baking paper over the top and then cover with foil and seal the edges.

Cook in the oven for 30–40 minutes, then pull the dish out, uncover and check. You want the potatoes to be just cooked through – test some of the potatoes in the middle with a skewer to make sure. If you are pre-preparing the dish, at this stage you can cool it and set it aside in the fridge until you are ready to serve. Just make sure to bring it to room temperature before you move on to the final stage.

Turn your oven up to 200°C (390°F). Once it comes up to temperature, put the potatoes back in and cook for a further 15–20 minutes. The potatoes should be crisp and starting to darken and bubbling away. Serve hot.

NOTE I use a curved oval baking dish (pictured), which is 25 cm (10 in) long x 15 cm (6 in) at its widest point. You will need something around this size; however, the recipe is easily adjusted to a bit bigger or smaller. The main aim is that your potatoes fit snugly. I would just make sure you have an extra potato or two on hand to ensure this happens.

With mussels

SERVES 2–4

This dish turns kiri hodi into an easy meal. Make it, throw in your mussels to gently open and you have a wonderful brothy, sweet and slightly salty mussel dish, perfect for an easy midweek meal or a lazy weekend lunch.

- 500 ml (17 fl oz) Kiri hodi (page 205)
- 1 kg (2 lb 3 oz) mussels
- olive oil, to drizzle
- side of rice, roti or bread, to serve
- coriander (cilantro), to garnish (optional)

Warm your kiri hodi in a large saucepan. Add in the mussels, cover with a lid and cook until the mussels just start to open.

Serve drizzled with olive oil and a side of rice, roti or bread. Coriander would be a nice garnish, if you felt the need.

And another not-quite-recipe, but a very good combination that we once did at LFS: miso, tomato, chicory and fried eggplant

This version is inspired by Japanese flavours. Simply make the kiri hodi as per normal but don't season with salt. Instead, once it's cooked, whisk in 30 g (1 oz) of white miso. Meanwhile on the side, blanch and peel 300 g (10½ oz) cherry tomatoes and add these to the kiri hodi. Cut 200 g (7 oz) of chicory into 3 cm (1¼ in) pieces, fry it off in a little ghee and then set aside. Get some eggplant (aubergine), cut it into bite-sized chunks, salt it for a moment and use the batter from the cuttlefish recipe (page 144) to deep-fry it.

Put the chicory in the base of the bowl, the eggplant on top and then spoon the kiri hodi over. This is a good side, but would work equally as well as a meal in itself. If you want to carry on with the Japanese theme, serve it as a noodle dish with some udon.

Dhal

SERVES 4–6

This recipe is a staple, both on the island and in my restaurant, and also exactly as written from LF. It's a perfect dish, warm, comforting, gentle, simple, healthful and delicious. That's all.

- **75 g (2¾ oz) coconut oil**
- **5 g (⅕ oz) picked curry leaves**
- **550 g (1 lb 3 oz) brown onions, cut into medium dice**
- **18 g (⅔ oz) finely chopped garlic**
- **15 g (½ oz) finely chopped ginger**
- **salt flakes and freshly ground black pepper**
- **7 g (¼ oz) black mustard seeds**
- **5 g (⅕ oz) turmeric powder**
- **1 cinnamon stick**
- **4 × 5 cm (2 in) pieces rampe (pandan) leaf**
- **bottom 5 cm (2 in) of 1 lemongrass stem, white part only, lightly bruised**
- **525 g (1 lb 3 oz) red lentils, thoroughly washed**
- **450 ml (15 fl oz) coconut cream**

Melt the coconut oil in a medium saucepan over a medium heat, add the curry leaves and cook, stirring, for a minute or so until the leaves are fried. Add the onion, garlic and ginger and cook, stirring occasionally, for 6–7 minutes, until the onion has softened. Lightly season with salt and pepper.

Add the mustard seeds, turmeric and cinnamon and cook, stirring, for 1–2 minutes, until the turmeric begins to catch on the bottom of the pan.

Add the rampe (pandan) leaf, lemongrass and lentils and give everything a good stir to combine. Pour in the coconut cream and 1 litre (36 fl oz) of water and mix well, then reduce the heat to low and simmer gently for 10–15 minutes, stirring occasionally. The dhal is ready when all the lentils have just given away and turned yellow, while still retaining a little texture. Re-season with salt and pepper and serve hot.

SWEET

TREATS

(AND CAKE)

I think it's safe to say that most Sri Lankans have a bit of a sweet tooth – not surprising, given that it's a country rich in sugary and flavourful tropical fruits, nature's natural dessert. There are also sweetmeats aplenty, bakery delights, and no afternoon cup of tea is complete without a piece of love cake or a ginger biscuit. Or buttercake. Or something something.

I myself have historically been more of a savoury person. Growing up, my favourite treat was a salty olive or a tart pickled onion. Then, at the very start of LFS, when we were busy with the boring paperwork, my mate Nickos (who was integral to that first bit) would inevitably say at some stage in the afternoon, 'It's time for a cup of tea and a piece of cake.' At first, I just wobbled my head in a noncommittal manner, but it is now something I live for. Which suits me very well in Sri Lanka, where cakes abound.

I know desserts are meant to be sweet, but even with my newfound love of cakes I still look for balance in taste and texture, and a little bit of spice. Coming at the end of the meal, they can be a bit tricky, as you are already probably quite full. This can be particularly true post a highly spiced Sri Lankan curry meal, when your palate can be overwhelmed and you need something a little bit more refreshing. In Sri Lanka though, post-meal desserts are often super sweet, and the excellent tropical fruits are often reserved for breakfast.

The recipes here mostly rely on Lankan flavours, but none are very traditional. We have a few fruity type dessert dishes, which would be my go-to after a heavy meal. There are a couple of chocolate things too – after all, who doesn't like chocolate? And of course, a couple of cakes and a tart, because even if you want to skip dessert, you'll still need something for your afternoon tea.

Strawberries, rose, pepperberry and whipped coconut

SERVES 4

If the flavour of rose was a person, she would be a diva. So overpowering is her scent that for one lovely lady I used to work with, even the slightest hint would make her weep with the memories it conjured. Luckily, rose can be wrangled into playing nicely with others, strawberries being one friendship that can wobble between perfection and sickly sweetness. This little combination harnesses the floral notes of both with some seasoning and a cooling, calming fluffy cloud of coconut. I'm sure others have done it, but when we first whipped some coconut cream at LFS we felt as if we'd discovered something special. It is such a simple thing, but is just as perfect as whipped cream, and in fact, combining the two creams is also very delicious. We have found that the brand of coconut cream you use does have a big impact here, as some just refuse to whip. And of course, to make this dish perfect, you will need the right kind of rose syrup (page 21) and for strawberries to be in season. When a dish is this simple, all the elements need to be correct.

- 200 ml (7 fl oz) coconut cream, cold
- 300g (10½ oz) ripe strawberries, at room temperature
- 1½ g ($\frac{1}{32}$ oz) salt flakes
- a sprinkle of ground pepperberry
- 80 ml (2½ fl oz) rose syrup

Whip your coconut cream with a hand blender or stand mixer until it forms soft peaks. This is easier and faster to do when the coconut cream is cold. Once whipped, store it in the fridge. You can do this in advance, it will last overnight, but may need a quick hand whisk to re-firm it a little.

Use a sharp paring knife to cut a little around the hull of the strawberry, removing the green. Then cut the strawberries in halves or quarters, depending on their size and what you think you want to spoon into your mouth.

Place them in a mixing bowl and season with the salt and pepperberry. Stir to combine, then pour over the syrup and mix again. Let this sit for about 5 minutes.

To serve, divide the strawberries between four little bowls or coupe dishes (a nice old-fashioned glass one works well here), evenly pouring in all of the syrup. Finish with a nice dollop of the cold coconut cream.

Melon, sago and pomelo

SERVES 6–8

I can't remember the original motivation for this dish as it was something from my time at Berta, and that was so long ago, but I still clearly remember tasting the finished dessert and thinking how much it tasted like bubble gum. It made me want to giggle with delight. This is a dish I love so much that I have kept it close, and it keeps appearing in various guises. This melon version is perfect for summer when the fruit is perfumed and sweet, but equally good, although fiddlier, is a winter version I have done with many types of citrus. And one time, as part of a collab dinner, we added a ginger granita on top. This is a dessert with flavours that could seamlessly blend into many parts of Asia. It's refreshing, cooling and fruity.

100 g (3½ oz) sago pearls

watermelon, about 200 g (7 oz) worth of balls

rockmelon, about 200 g (7 oz) worth of balls

honeydew, about 200 g (7 oz) worth of balls

1 large pomelo

coconut cream, to serve

SYRUP

300 g (10½ oz) caster (superfine) sugar

1 vanilla pod, split and scraped

½ cinnamon stick

2 fresh bay leaves

3 sprigs curry leaves, picked

1 rampe (pandan) leaf, tied

3 g (1⁄10 oz) cooking salt

a tiny splash of rosewater

1 lemongrass stalk, set aside the bottom 5 cm (2 in) and cut the remaining bit of the stalk into 5 cm (2 in) pieces to use

To make the syrup, place the sugar in a large saucepan with 450 ml (15 fl oz) of water and bring to a boil over a medium heat. Add in the remaining syrup ingredients and simmer gently for 5 minutes. The syrup will look nice and thick. Set aside to cool and then refrigerate until it's properly cold. Make sure to strain the syrup before you start adding anything else to it.

For the sago, bring 1 litre (34 fl oz) of water to a rolling boil and salt it slightly. Slowly pour in the sago, boil for 7 minutes and then remove from the heat and cover with a lid. Let this sit for 20 minutes by which stage the sago should be ready and completely translucent. Strain through a fine strainer, rinse under cold water and add to your cold, strained sugar syrup.

To prepare your melons, find a small baller and use it to make little melon balls, reserving any juice. You want to end up with roughly equal amounts of each type of melon. Add the balls and any stray melon juice to the syrup with the sago.

To prepare your pomelo, cut away the outside skin and then separate the segments from the pith. A paring knife is best for this job. You want to separate the segments into small, bite-sized pieces no bigger than your melon balls. Add this to the mix as well.

Once everything is in, put your mixture back into the fridge. It's best if it sits overnight, and will also last a good 3 days in the fridge.

Serve this soupy dessert straight from the fridge. Give it a nice mix to ensure each bowl has a bit of everything. Serve it with some nice coconut cream on the side, whipped or not.

Mango fool

SERVES 6

I have always loved a fool. They're so light and fluffy and seem insubstantial in a good way. Raspberries were always my go-to fruit for this dessert until one summer when we had friends coming over and some spare mangoes in the fridge. And then this happened. I was quite pleased, as I had been searching for a mango dessert for the restaurant. Mangoes are so perfect as is, it can seem silly to prod them into something complicated. I think this is a nice compromise though, with very few ingredients. A traditional fool is cream alone, but I like the addition of yoghurt as it adds a hint of sourness. The layer of brown sugar on top is a trick I stole from Chazzy and it adds the right amount of extra sweet and a little texture. Like the strawberries before, this is another simple fruit dessert that's perfect after a heavy meal. It's also good for breakfast.

- 2 whole large mangoes, perfectly ripe but still a little firm, approximately 420 g (15 oz) each
- 400 ml (13½ fl oz) thickened (double/heavy) cream
- 200 g (7 oz) thick yoghurt
- 100 g (3½ oz) dark brown sugar

Cut the cheeks off your mangoes and use a large spoon to scoop out the flesh. Cut two of the cheeks into 2 mm (1⁄16 in) slices along the short side and set aside in a bowl in the fridge. Place the remaining cheeks in a blender along with all the mango flesh from around the seeds. I cut away as much as I can and then, over a bowl or on a board, use a spoon to scrape off the rest. Blend until smooth.

Using a whisk, a hand blender or a stand mixer, whip the cream until you have firm peaks. A whisk is the harder way of doing this, but it will also give you the most control, and doesn't really take that long as it's not a lot of cream. Also, it's good exercise.

Add in the yoghurt and use a spatula to gently but thoroughly combine. Add the mango puree and slices to the bowl, making sure to separate and scatter the mango slices. Again, gently combine with the spatula. It doesn't need to be fully incorporated, as you want streaky bits of the puree through the dessert.

Spoon the mix into a large shallow bowl (a nice glass one does look pretty for this), cover with a beeswax wrap or plastic wrap and set in the fridge for at least 6 hours or overnight.

About 2 hours before serving, remove your fool from the fridge and sprinkle over the sugar to form a thick even layer across the top. Cover, then return to the fridge for 2 hours.

Serve cold, straight from the fridge.

Chocolate and kithul fudge sundae

MAKES 330 ML (11½ FL OZ) CHOCOLATE SAUCE AND ENOUGH BITS FOR 6 GENEROUS SUNDAES

Back in the day when I didn't care for sweets, the thought of making a sundae would never have crossed my mind. It wasn't even something I had ever eaten. But I was in the midst of an obsession with combining cardamom and chocolate when I discovered that kithul, with its smoky, savoury ways, was a fine addition to the mix. I needed a conduit, and so turned to the classic chocolate fudge sundae and imposed this excellent flavour combination upon it, adding coconut too, as we are Sri Lankan after all. And this dessert now suits me just fine with its mix of textures and salty sweetness.

- **120 g (4½ oz) whole raw skinned peanuts**
- **salt flakes**
- **80 g (2¾ oz) coconut flakes**
- **150 ml (5 fl oz) coconut cream, cold**
- **good quality vanilla ice cream or gelato, to serve, 1 large scoop per person**
- **kithul, to serve, at least 120 ml (4 fl oz)**

CHOCOLATE SAUCE

- **100 g (3½ oz) dark chocolate (70 per cent cocoa), cut into pieces**
- **130 ml (4½ fl oz) pouring (single/light) cream, plus 30 ml (1 fl oz) more**
- **70 g (2½ oz) condensed milk**
- **3 g (1/10 oz) ground cardamom**
- **salt flakes**

Preheat the oven to 150°C (300°F). Toast your peanuts on a tray lined with baking paper for 10–12 minutes, until they are nicely cooked to an even golden brown. Remove from the oven, season with a little salt and then cool. Once cool, use a mortar and pestle to crush them ever so slightly. Set aside.

Toast your coconut flakes in the same oven for 7–9 minutes, until they are a similar golden brown. You will need to shake them a few times to ensure even cooking. Set aside to cool.

Whip your coconut cream in a stand mixer to soft peaks. Set aside in the fridge until ready to construct.

Melt the chocolate and first batch of cream gently together in a metal bowl over a double boiler. Whisk until smooth.

Meanwhile, gently warm the condensed milk and the other measure of cream together in a small saucepan.

Once the chocolate is smooth and the condensed milk mix is warm, whisk to combine, adding in the cardamom and salt. This sauce is best served just warm or at room temperature. If you are not going to use it immediately, you can re-warm it gently in a bowl over a double boiler.

Once all your elements are ready you can start sundae construction. A glass coupe is ideal for this, otherwise any old bowl will do.

Start with a good amount of chocolate sauce, lining the sides and the base of your bowl. Lay in a scoop of your gelato or ice cream, add a sprinkle of nuts and then drizzle over some kithul. Cover this with some whipped coconut and then top with another sprinkle of the nuts and the coconut flakes. Finish it all with an extra drizzle of kithul and serve immediately.

Chocolate and arrack mousse cake

MAKES 1 LARGE CAKE, 25 CM (10 IN)

I first made this so long ago its origins are lost to the mists of time, but I am fairly sure it was a straight-up steal from the internet. However, after countless variations I am happy to claim it enough to share it with you all. This is an easy cake to make – there's no real cooking involved – with very few ingredients, and it can be hustled up in no time, although it does need to set. It's vegan friendly, if that's your sort of thing, and almost completely sugar free, the only sweetness coming from the final dusting of icing sugar to serve. The beauty of this cake lies in its texture, and the key to getting this right is the whipping of the coconut. Tame that part properly and you'll have something soft and light yet not insubstantial. If you do have trouble sourcing a coconut cream that whips nicely, you can make the cake with normal cream.

- 10 black peppercorns
- 1 cinnamon stick, broken up into pieces
- ½ g ($\frac{1}{16}$ oz) fennel seeds
- 1.2 g ($\frac{1}{32}$ oz) cloves
- 3 whole cardamom pods
- 200 ml (7 fl oz) coconut cream, plus 800 ml (2½ fl oz) more, cold
- 60 ml (2 fl oz) arrack
- 400 g (14 oz) dark chocolate (70 per cent cocoa), chopped
- 6 g ($\frac{1}{5}$ oz) cocoa nibs
- a small handful of icing (confectioners') sugar, for dusting
- 200 ml (7 fl oz) extra whipped coconut cream, or whipped cream, to serve

Place all the spices in a small frying pan over a medium heat and gently toast for 1 minute. Remove from the heat, then use a mortar and pestle to break them up slightly.

Transfer to a small saucepan with the first batch of coconut cream and 200 ml (7 oz) of water and place over a medium heat. Be careful, as once it comes to a boil it tends to overflow. Gently reduce over a low heat for about 5 minutes, until the mixture becomes thick and creamy. It will go dark and may split; don't worry. Strain the spices through a fine strainer into a bowl, pressing down to get as much liquid as you can. You should be left with about 150 ml (5 fl oz).

To this, add the arrack, then place in the fridge to cool.

Grease the base and side of a 25 cm (10 in) springform cake tin, then line the base with plastic wrap.

Whisk the cold coconut cream in a stand mixer on medium speed until you have soft peaks. Leave the cream in the mixing bowl and rest it in the fridge for about 30 minutes until it sets a little.

Melt the chocolate in a double boiler.

Return the bowl with the coconut cream to the stand mixer and beat on medium speed as you pour the melted chocolate over the cream, followed by the cold arrack mix. This will only take a few moments, by which stage your cream will be at soft peaks again. Don't overwhip or you'll end up with a gritty texture. This can't be fixed ...

Stop the mixer and use a spatula to give the mix a final turn, making sure to get any last bits of chocolate from the bottom. Transfer the mix to the prepared tin and gently tap it to smooth the top (be careful not to flip the clasp on your springform pan – if your tin opens it can ruin everything). Sprinkle with the cocoa nibs before covering with plastic wrap and placing in the fridge for at least 5 hours to set.

To serve, remove the cake from the tin, being careful to ease it off the plastic wrap on the base. Heavily dust the top of the cake with icing sugar and serve slices with a generous blob of whipped cream.

Spiced jaggery custard tart

MAKES ONE 27 CM (10¾ IN) TART

This tart is inspired by the Sri Lankan-spiced custard dessert, wattalappam. It's a very traditional dessert made with jaggery and cooked until firm, giving it a weird eggy texture. The recipe I use is exactly as my Nan taught me, but I cook it far less and more gently to give a silky texture and serve it in bowls. Here is a tart version, which is equally as good.

- **350 g (12½ oz) jaggery, coarsely grated**
- **1 vanilla bean, split and scraped**
- **2.7 g (1⁄10 oz) ground cardamom**
- **1.5 g (1⁄32 oz) ground cinnamon**
- **4 g (⅛ oz) cooking salt**
- **20 ml (¾ fl oz) rosewater**
- **8 egg yolks**
- **2.7 g (1⁄10 oz) grated nutmeg**
- **400 ml (13½ fl oz) coconut cream**

PASTRY

- **10 ml (¼ fl oz) white vinegar**
- **260 g (9 oz) plain (all-purpose) flour**
- **30 g (1 oz) caster (superfine) sugar**
- **115 g (4 oz) unsalted butter, diced and cold**
- **70 g (2½ oz) mascarpone**
- **1 egg, lightly beaten**

NOTE You can very easily break tart-making down into stages for ease. The pastry can be made up to a week in advance and kept in the fridge, but it also freezes very well. And the rolling and baking of the tart shell can also be done in stages, as once baked, the shell will last for a good few days. This means all the hard pastry work can be done prior, ready for you to slip the custard in and have a lovely tart, ready to be eaten from the oven in no time.

To make the pastry, combine the vinegar with 15 ml (½ fl oz) of water and place in the fridge to cool.

Combine the flour and sugar and, using either your hands or a blender, add in the butter and combine until the mix resembles breadcrumbs.

Add in the vinegar water and mascarpone and use your hands to gently bring the pastry mix together without working it too much. Don't worry if it looks a little streaky.

Shape the pastry into a disc, wrap with plastic wrap and rest in the fridge for at least 6 hours; overnight is better.

Lightly grease a 27 cm (10¾ in) round tart tin.

On a floured surface, roll out the pastry to a circle a little larger than the tart tin, about 3 mm (⅛ in) thick. Line your tin with the pastry, making sure to press the edges in firmly and hopefully leaving some overhang around the edges. Prick the base of the tart shell with a fork and place in the fridge or a freezer to rest. It will need about 2 hours in the freezer and at least 5 hours in the fridge.

Preheat the oven to 180°C (360°F).

Once rested, place a sheet of baking paper over your pastry and weigh it down with pastry weights, rice or beans and blind bake for 30 minutes. Remove the tart shell from the oven, drop the temperature to 160°C (320°C) and remove your baking weights and the baking paper. Return to the oven and cook for a further 20–25 minutes, turning to make sure it cooks evenly. I like quite a dark cook on my pastry.

Remove the shell from the oven and brush the insides with the beaten egg, then cook for a further 5 minutes. If you are not going to bake your tart immediately, save this last step until you are.

To make the filling, combine the jaggery, spices and rosewater with 250 ml (8½ fl oz) of water in a small saucepan. Warm over a medium heat, whisking until the jaggery dissolves. Remove from the heat and allow to cool to room temperature.

In a medium mixing bowl, whisk together the yolks and the nutmeg until well combined, then pour in the jaggery mix, still gently whisking as you go. Continue this process with the coconut cream. This is a gentle whisk, just to combine the ingredients. Strain the mixture through a fine strainer and set aside.

Reduce your oven temperature to 140°C (285°F).

Carefully pour your custard mix into the still-warm pastry shell and bake until the custard is only just set – it should still have a nice wobble in the middle if you jiggle it. This will take between 40–50 minutes depending on your oven, and you will probably need to give the tart a turn halfway through cooking. Turn the heat off and leave the tart in the oven for another 30 minutes or so to fully set before removing.

Allow to cool to room temperature before slicing and serving. It isn't entirely necessary, but the tart does go well with an extra blob of mascarpone, or even a little whipped cream or coconut cream.

Spiced kithul cake

MAKES
1 LARGE CAKE,
FEEDS 16–20

This beauty came about when I wanted to bake a very special birthday cake. I asked Muu what kind I should do and he said a Russian honey cake, something I knew nothing about. Being dutiful, however, I read many recipes and, being me, decided to not quite follow any of them properly, instead producing a hybrid. Luckily it was a great success. I found myself smitten, and knew I wanted more. Tampering with it enough to move from Russia to Sri Lanka, I added a little extra spice and transitioned from honey to kithul. The kithul is an easy substitute that brings an inherent smokiness and depth. And so, many experiments later, this excellent cake appeared on the menu at LFS. It is definitely time-consuming and fiddly, and the recipe sounds a bit complicated, but the actual technique is not too hard to master. You just have concentrate and, like I do even now, make sure you read the recipe several times before you attempt it. I find it easiest if you measure out all the cake ingredients before you start. Traditionally made as a round, we started doing this as a rectangle, which gives lovely long fancy looking slices when you cut it. To do this, however, you will need to use a ruler to measure your rectangles onto baking paper. If you think you will attempt it many more times, make a template for ease. It's worth investing in a small crank-handled palette knife to make this, a handy kitchen tool that is one of my favourites.

CAKE

340 ml (11½ oz) kithul

230 g (8 oz) caster (superfine) sugar

200 g (7 oz) unsalted butter, diced

6 large eggs, gently whisked together

12 g (½ oz) bicarbonate of soda (baking soda)

2 g (1⁄16 oz) ground cardamom

2 g (1⁄16 oz) ground cinnamon

1 g (1⁄32 oz) ground clove

5 g (1⁄5 oz) cooking salt

460 g (1 lb) plain (all-purpose) flour, sifted

160 g (5½ oz) fresh grated coconut

Start by ruling out your cake stencils onto sheets of baking paper. You will need ten sheets, each with a rectangle 18 × 24 cm (7 × 9½ in). I find a pencil is good for this; make sure you rule good sharp dark lines. Set aside.

To make the cake, combine the kithul, sugar and butter in a large mixing bowl and place the bowl over a saucepan of simmering water. Once the butter has melted, whisk to combine.

Keeping the bowl over the heat, add in the eggs and whisk to combine for a minute, then add the bicarb, spices and salt and whisk again. The mixture should go a little foamy. Keep whisking for 1 minute in total.

Remove the bowl from above the water, give it a minute to cool slightly and then whisk in the flour in a few batches. You will end up with a sticky batter.

Preheat the oven to 180°C (360°F).

Your cake layers will need to be baked in batches. If you have enough trays, you should be able to do about three layers at a time.

Place one of your stencils, pencil-side down, onto a baking tray and add a little masking tape on each edge to secure it onto the tray. If you can, measure out 120 g (4½ oz) cake batter into the middle of the stencil and use a crank-handled pallet knife to spread the mixture into a nice sharp rectangle, sitting evenly and nicely within your stencil. This can be a bit fiddly and tricky, but the more precisely you can do it, the better the end result will be.

Repeat this twice more, then place the three trays in the oven to bake for 7–8 minutes, until the cakes are a deep brown colour and spring back to the touch. Remove from the oven and gently transfer each cake to a wire rack.

Keep going to the best of your capacity until you have ten nice cake layers. If the trays are going back in hot, you may need to lessen the cooking time by a minute or so.

At the end of this you will have some batter left over. Spread this evenly but not necessarily neatly onto a final sheet of baking paper,

CREAM

- 1½ titanium gelatine leaves (7.8 g/ ¼ oz)
- 170 ml (5 ½ fl oz) kithul
- 380 g (13½ oz) dulce de leche (see Notes)
- 3 g (⅒ oz) cooking salt
- 900 ml (30½ fl oz) pouring cream
- 330 g (11½ oz) sour cream
- 300 g (10½ oz) cream cheese, at room temperature

lower the oven temperature to 150°C (300°F) and bake this layer for about 20–25 minutes, until it is completely dried out.

Leaving the oven at the same temperature, spread your grated coconut onto another baking tray and toast in the oven for about 10–15 minutes, mixing it around every 5 minutes or so, until it becomes a nice golden brown colour.

Allow this final cake layer and the coconut to cool completely before combining in a blender and blitzing to a fine crumb. Set this aside for cake decorating.

While your cakes cool, make the cream. If you prefer, this can be made the day before and left to sit in the fridge.

Place the gelatine in cold water to soften, and warm the kithul in a small pan. Once the gelatine has softened, remove the kithul from the heat and whisk in the gelatine.

In a small mixing bowl, whisk together the kithul, dulce de leche and salt until well combined. Sit this in the fridge to cool.

Once it has cooled, gently whisk in half of the cream and all of the sour cream until just combined. Set aside.

Place the cream cheese in a bowl of a stand mixer and use a spatula to soften until it becomes a smooth paste. Slowly whisk in the remaining cream. You need to do this gently until the mix is fully combined, then start whisking in earnest to achieve soft peaks. Once you have nice soft peaks, gradually whisk in the other kithul cream until you have firm peaks and the mix looks silky. The texture of this is crucial. You don't want lumps (no one likes lumpy cream), it can't be too soft or you'll have issues building your cake, and if it's too firm it runs the risk of splitting and losing its firmness.

Store the cream mix in the fridge until you are ready to build.

Lay your first cake layer, top-side down onto the plate or board you wish to serve your cake on. Measure out about 80 g (3 oz) of your cream mix and use your handy palette knife to evenly spread the cream mix right to the edges. Place another layer of cake on top and gently press it down so it's sitting flat. Repeat this process with all ten layers of cake. I would suggest weighing each batch of cream as you go for consistency.

Once you have finished constructing your cake you will have ample cream mix left to cover the entire cake, sides and all. Once completely covered, get your coconut crumb mix and pat it along the sides and top to decorate. The cake will then need to be covered however you see fit and left to sit in the fridge overnight.

To serve, cut nice long thin slices across the cake. Nothing else is needed.

NOTES To make the dulche de leche, place a tin of condensed milk into a saucepan of cold water, bring to a boil over a medium heat, then simmer gently for 3 hours (don't accidentally leave it on overnight like I once did, it will explode ...). Keep the water level topped up so it covers the can. Once it has cooked long enough, leave the can in the water to cool before removing from the pan and letting it cool completely.

Let's talk about the curiosity of gelatine measures which are given as a powder measurement or as leaves, either silver, gold or titanium. Firstly, I know nothing about powdered gelatin so I can't help you there but what I did learn in the not-so-distant past is that the reference to leaves is merely an indication of weight. So if you are using a recipe and don't have the leaves specified you can just work it out according to weight. This was a revelation to me.

Chocolates

Here's a sweeping statement: most traditional Asian desserts don't involve chocolate. The hot and humid weather of many tropical Asian countries doesn't really lend itself to the keeping of chocolates, nor to the making of them. It would be a bit like trying to temper a chocolate bar in a tiny, hot, busy kitchen at the beginning of service, which is actually how this coconut and chocolate bar first came to be. Anyhow, I digress. The point, I think, is that chocolate is always good, and deserves a place even on the menu of a Sri Lankan restaurant. So here we have two recipes, one with coconut, these two friends being a fine combination, and both with cardamom, as this is my current favourite flavour combination. Both of these require tempering, a bit of a process, for which I give brief and shallow directions. These should get you by, but if you want to get really involved, I would suggest reading more about it, as it's a clever science. You will need an electric probe thermometer to make these, and a heatproof spatula is also good. And my best tip is to make sure you are well prepared and neat, otherwise you'll end up with chocolate everywhere. I am not a chocolatier, my knowledge is rudimentary, so if I can do it, so can you.

LFS bounty

MAKES 30 BARS

You will need a tin to set this in. I use one around 20 x 30 cm (8 x 12 in), which will make your chocolate bars a nice height, but a few centimetres here or there won't make much of a difference.

- 15 g (½ oz) puffed rice or rice flakes
- 80 g (2¾ oz) buckwheat
- 250 g (9 oz) milk chocolate (33 per cent cocoa), in buttons or cut into small pieces
- 130 g (4½ oz) pouring (single/light) cream
- 110 g (4 oz) fresh grated coconut
- 390 g (14 oz) dark chocolate (70 per cent cocoa), in buttons or finely chopped
- salt flakes
- finely ground cardamon seeds

Grease and line your tin neatly with baking paper.

Lightly toast your puffed rice or rice flakes in a frying pan over a gentle heat for about 2–3 minutes, until they crisp a little. Transfer to a bowl and set aside to cool.

Do the same with your buckwheat, this will take about the same amount of time. Once toasted, add it to your rice.

Combine the milk chocolate and cream in a metal bowl and place over a saucepan of gently simmering water. Use a spatula to stir and melt. As soon as all the chocolate is melted, remove the bowl from the heat and add in the fresh coconut along with your toasted bits. Mix well to combine.

Pour your chocolate mix into your tin. Bang the tin on the bench, then smooth with the spatula to ensure the surface is nice and flat. Set in the fridge for at least 5 hours or overnight. This will be the inside of your chocolate bar.

Once your chocolate has set, turn it out from the tin and cut it into thirty equal bars. If your tin is the exact size I use, the bars should each measure 6 cm × 3 cm (2½ × 1¼ in). Place the bars on a tray and keep them in the fridge while you prepare your temper.

Before you start the temper, make sure you have a nice clear surface. Have two forks at hand, which you will use to dip your bars. Place the salt flakes and ground cardamom in small ramekins, ready to season as you go, and have another baking paper-lined tray or two, big enough to lay your completed bars on with space between them. Set up a saucepan of simmering water – it should accommodate your chocolate-melting bowl allowing it to sit on top without touching the water. You will also need your thermometer, and a damp sponge for wiping (but remember, no water in the actual chocolate, as they are enemies in this process).

Okay, ready?

Place 260 g (9 oz) of your dark chocolate into a heatproof bowl. Place it over the simmering water and use your spatula to mix it as it melts. Keep mixing, you want this to happen evenly until your chocolate reaches between 55°–58°C (131–136°F). This will take about 3–4 minutes.

Remove from the heat, add in the remaining 130 g (4½ oz) chocolate and keep mixing. The aim here is for the rest of the chocolate to melt, cooling the mixture in the process. Keep working the chocolate until the temperature drops to 28–29°C (82–84°F). This might take longer than you expect, up to 10 minutes. You will notice that the chocolate starts to thicken.

Once you reach this temperature, place the bowl back on the saucepan of simmering water, only briefly, and still stirring constantly. You need to heat the chocolate back up but only by a few degrees, to between 31–32°C (87–89°F). When it hits this point, the chocolate will suddenly loosen and become fluid again. It should look nice and shiny.

At this point you need to move swiftly. Rest the bowl of tempered chocolate on a tea towel (dish towel) in front of you. Lower a chocolate bar into the mix and then use a fork in each hand to pull it out again. Have one fork underneath the bar, holding it, and use the other to tap against the holding fork to knock off as much excess chocolate as you can. Gently lower the bar onto your waiting tray, remove the fork and season with a sprinkle of salt and a more generous sprinkle of cardamom. Do this quickly, before the chocolate sets.

Now it's just a matter of repeating this process with the remaining bars. Check the temperature of your chocolate every few bars to make sure it's still sitting around the 31–32°C (87–89°F) mark. You should be able to tell if it's cooled too much, as the chocolate will become less liquid. Just slip it back over the heat for a few seconds to get it back to where it should be.

Once all your bars are coated, store them in the fridge until they are properly set. Once they set, you are safe to pick them up and store them in a container, although I would still keep them in the fridge.

You know you have had success if the chocolate is shiny and without streaks. When you bite into a bar it should not be too thick and should have a nice snap. If this isn't the case, that means something went wrong in temper land and you will need to try again one day. The bars will still taste delicious though.

These can be stored in the fridge for ages.

Chocolate and cardamom truffles

MAKES 20

These little balls are similar in flavour to the LFS bounty but are a bit more delicate, simple and bite-sized. Make sure to use a very good quality virgin coconut oil, otherwise the taste can be overpowering. If you don't like that coconut oil flavour, substitute with butter.

- 250 g (9 oz) milk chocolate (30 per cent cocoa), in buttons or cut into small pieces
- 130 g (4½ oz) pouring (single/light) cream
- 30 g (1 oz) coconut oil
- 5 g (⅕ oz) cooking salt
- 3 g (⅒ oz) finely ground cardamom seeds
- 210 g (7½ oz) dark chocolate (70 per cent cocoa), in buttons or finely chopped
- approximately 60 g (2 oz) dark cocoa powder, sifted

Place all the ingredients up to the cardamom into a metal bowl and melt, stirring as you go, over a saucepan of simmering water.

Remove the bowl from the heat and let the mixture come to room temperature before placing it in the fridge to set. This is your ganache, which is ready to use as soon as it's set enough for you to scoop.

Once you are ready to roll, remove the ganache from the fridge and use a tablespoon measure to scoop out the mix into even portions, about 20 g (¾ oz) per piece. Roll each portion into a nice ball using your hands, then place on a tray or plate. This step can get messy and may require a bit of shuffling as you may need to pop the chocolate in and out of the fridge as you go to find the ideal rolling temperature. Too cold makes it hard to roll, but too warm and the chocolate will just melt. You need to work swiftly and having cold hands helps.

Once all your balls are rolled you have two options. You can skip the whole tempering step and instead, lay all your balls onto a tray and heavily dust them with the sifted cocoa powder, jiggling them as you go to cover completely.

Once covered, place them on the tray into the fridge to set. Once set, you can store them a container in the fridge.

However, if you do want to go the extra step and temper, refer to the LFS bounty bar recipe (page 235) and follow the steps for tempering and coating. The only difference is you will need less chocolate (melt 140 g/5 oz first, then add the remaining 70 g/2½ oz) and you won't need to season the balls with salt and cardamom. Once the balls are all coated and on a tray, sift the cocoa powder over the top and jiggle your tray to completely coat them. Again, store them in the fridge.

Once your truffles are made, whichever version you have gone with, they will last happily and nicely in the fridge for ages, if you actually manage to not eat them all by then.

DRINKS

THE BOOZY AND THE NOT

LFS started life as an idea of a small, simple kade (shop), focused on hoppers, with quality ingredients but fast and simple. More street food and less restauranty. That was until the day I decided I needed a martini on the menu. This one drink shifted the whole idea, and suddenly I was building a proper restaurant. And so, I had to have a proper drinks menu, one that would match the food, obviously.

When I'm on the island my non-alcoholic choices are thambali, a lime soda or ginger beer. At LFS, we had a ginger beer that despite being made in New Zealand did actually use Lankan ginger (and is delightfully spicy), but apart from that, all our sodas were made in-house and our coconut water came from mature coconuts that we bought in to grate. Our soda section became quite large, mostly using by-products from the food menu.

But a sparkling cold drink is a great way to combat heat. As is a lassi – we always had a seasonal one on the menu, its yoghurt coolness is one of the best ways to dampen the heat. There is tea and coffee too, of course, and a few drinks that lean into these flavours.

To the booze, beer is the obvious match, and is something I drink more in Sri Lanka than I ever do here. What about wine, though? The whole idea of matching wines to a curry meal does tend to throw people, as it feels like it doesn't make sense. The island doesn't have a history of wine making, and the chilli and high spice levels of the food arguably render the subtle flavours of this grape product pointless. While this can be true of some, like any food and wine match, you just need to find the right one. I like to think we had a nice little list of wines that suited our food, so please don't be scared to explore this idea further.

Spirits and cocktails are another fun thing to play with. As partial as I am to a cocktail, I am also very particular. I tend to stick to the classics – a martini is my forever go-to – and mostly avoid the others. That said, I am about to present you with some that are only very slight twists on classics. If you are not a beer drinker and you remain unconvinced of my argument about wine and curries, then perhaps you should just go ahead and drink these cocktails with all the recipes from this book. It would not be a terrible idea.

Sodas

If you hang out in restaurants, particularly in Australia, you may have noticed that over the last decade the non-alcoholic drink options have just kept increasing. Fancy restaurants doing degustation menus now nearly always offer a non-booze match, or even a mixed match (half booze, half not, which I think is very clever and is my go-to), and there are many bars popping up with not a skerrick of alcohol in sight. It feels like collectively, humans are growing up and realising the sad truth that too much booze is not good for you, and does in fact make you feel bad. I have been in denial about this for a long time as I am fond of a tipple, but the more I abstain, the more I realise how much it affects me. The good news, though, is that non-alcoholic beverages are now much more sophisticated than your average soft drink. Among the selection we offered at LFS were our house sodas. Some were made purposefully, while others came about as a way to use up by-products of other dishes on the menu.

Salted cucumber

MAKES 1 SODA

For those of you who spend time at day spas, airport lounges or fancy hotels, this will likely be a familiar flavour to you, just a little more savoury. Our version happened because of our cucumber raita – it is made using the slightly green, slightly salted liquid left over after squeezing out the cucumber. A staff member added it to her water bottle one day and suddenly we had a new drink on the menu. It is subtle yet refreshing, and a perfect cooling beverage to go with spicy food, just like the raita that you'll need to make first.

- 30–50 ml (1–1¾ fl oz) cucumber water (leftover from making Raita, see page 45)
- 200 ml (7 fl oz) sparkling water or soda
- cucumber slices, to garnish
- ice

Place half the cucumber water in a glass half filled with ice. Add the cucumber slices, top with sparkling water and then pour in the remaining cucumber water. Stir and drink.

Sparkling rose

MAKES 1 SODA

We always have rose syrup to hand as it is the essential ingredient in our faluda, and at some stage we started finding other uses for it. I think it was the need to keep a small child happy that saw it turned into one of our sodas, but it also became a very handy mid-service pick-me-up drink for the wait staff. This is heading into slightly sickly-sweet territory, so make sure you get the ratios right and stir well, otherwise you could send yourself into a sugar coma. But the sweetness does work well with very hot food. The other essential thing here is to get the right rose syrup. Delicious is my preferred brand (also, with a name like that, who is to argue with it?).

- 20 ml (¾ fl oz) rose syrup
- 200 ml (7 fl oz) sparkling water or soda
- ice

Place half the rose syrup in a glass half filled with ice. Add the sparkling water and then pour in the remaining rose syrup. Stir and drink.

Fruit syrup

MAKES 1 SODA

When we cook fruit to make a lassi puree we sometimes end up with an excess of flavoured sugar syrup, which lends itself perfectly to becoming a soda. This recipe uses our clementine and star anise syrup as an example, but go wild with any fruit syrups you may have around. The amount of syrup will vary depending on the fruit and how concentrated it is.

- 30 ml (1 fl oz) clementine syrup (leftover from making lassi, see page 250)
- 200 ml (7 fl oz) sparkling water or soda
- clementine or orange peel, to garnish
- ice

Place half the syrup in a glass half filled with ice. Twist and add the peel, top with sparkling water and then pour in the remaining syrup. Stir and drink.

Lime soda

MAKES 1 SODA

When I'm in Sri Lanka my go-to non-boozy drinks are thambali, tea and lime soda. I have my tea black with lime and my lime soda with lime (obviously). Lankan limes are small but very juicy, strongly limey and delicious. When you get a lime soda in Sri Lanka it usually has a little salt added, which helps the body with rehydration, much needed when things are always so hot and sweaty. And, when you order one, you always get a little sugar syrup on the side so you can tailor the sweetness to your liking. You too can do this if my version isn't sweet enough for your taste.

- 50 ml (1¾ fl oz) lime juice
- 10 g (⅓ oz) caster (super fine) sugar
- 2 g (1/16 oz) cooking salt
- 200 ml (7 fl oz) sparkling water or soda
- ice
- lime wedge, to garnish

Place the lime juice, sugar and salt in a glass and stir until the sugar and salt have dissolved. Add some ice, a lime wedge and top with sparkling water.

Others, made in the same manner as the rose soda

Pepper soda

- 30 ml (1 fl oz) Black pepper syrup (page 257)
- 200 ml (7 fl oz) sparkling water or soda
- ice

Pineapple shrub soda

- 30 ml (a fl oz) Pineapple shrub (see page 258)
- 200 ml (7 fl oz) sparkling water or soda
- ice

Lassis

India is the origin of many Western trends, some of which have gotten a little out of hand: for example, yoga and a lassi, which is clearly the first iteration of lycra-clad ladies stretching out and then reaching for a smoothie. Incidentally, these are both things that I love (and participate in), but you know what I mean when I hint at its faddishness ... The original lassi is made with yoghurt and water blended with spices or fruits, and can be sweet or savoury. It is a wonderfully cooling drink, and while not as popular in Sri Lanka as India, I firmly feel it has a place here. The most common type is probably a mango lassi, which is interesting, as it's the one I least like having on the menu. You really need the right type of mango to make it: sweet, almost fermented in flavour and strong enough to stand up to the yoghurt. Late in the season, when there's a glut, is the best time to test this one, but there are so many less obvious flavour options. Not so common outside of India is the salted lassi, which is perfect with hot and spicy foods. We had it on the menu at LFS for a while but sadly the fact that I loved it didn't translate to sales. We always had a sweet lassi on the menu, which changed with the seasons. It was made with some sort of cooked fruit, which is a great way to dial up the intensity of the flavour, paired with a spice and pureed.

The following recipes below specify more fruit than is needed for one drink, but the purees are perfect for freezing and can then be used at whim whenever the lassi craving strikes. Once you have made your puree, the actual lassi making bit is easy and mostly the same for all, though you may need to adjust the puree amount depending on how flavourful your fruit is.

Lassi base (for all the sweet ones)

MAKES 1 LASSI

This is the base of all LFS lassis, the only difference being that we adjusted the amount of puree depending on its flavour, and sometimes we added a squirt of kithul to give an extra hint of sweetness. The coconut water is there to aid in the blending, but a splash of water works almost as well. We made ours in a small drinks blender, which is perfect for making one drink per person, but you can just adapt and scale up depending on what type of blender you have and whether you are going solo or making one for all your yoga mates.

- 80 g (2¾ oz) thick Greek yoghurt
- 160 g (5½) ice
- 80–120 g (2¾–4½ oz) puree (depending on the fruit)
- 30 ml (1 fl oz) coconut water or water

Combine all the ingredients in a blender and blitz well until smooth. Taste, and add a little more puree if needed. If you think it needs a bit more sweetness, a little kithul is a good addition.

Salted

MAKES 1 LASSI

This is one for the savoury lovers among us and uses a coconut yoghurt, which has the benefit of being dairy free if you are that way inclined (substitute a thick Greek yoghurt if the coconut variety doesn't tickle your fancy). Just steer clear of any brands that contain added sweetness, or you will be in for a very confusing 'am I sweet or am I savoury?' drinking moment.

- 150 g (5½ oz) unsweetened coconut yoghurt
- 70 ml (2¼ fl oz) coconut water
- ½ g (1/64 oz) cumin seeds, toasted and ground
- 2 g (1/16 oz) cooking salt
- 140 g (5 oz) ice

Add the yoghurt, coconut water, half the cumin, salt and ice to a blender and blitz well until smooth. Pour into a glass and serve with an extra sprinkle of cumin on top.

Grown-up

This was one of those secret items on our drinks list and seems to be good with most flavours. Just add two shots of arrack per lassi recipe and divide into two glasses, one for you and one for a friend. It's very good for a brunch time treat.

Clementine and star anise

MAKES 700 G (1 LB 9 OZ)

This puree is an old favourite which I love, mandarins being high on my list of perfect fruits. Cooked whole this way, you get a deep fruit flavour, and the sweetness is balanced out with the bitterness from the peel. Over time, many versions of this puree have appeared in all the restaurants in our family, sometimes sweet, like in a sorbet and often savoury, like as a base for a salad. Most varieties of mandarin can be substituted here, as can oranges and blood oranges.

250 g (9 oz) caster (superfine) sugar

2 whole star anise

600 g (1 lb 5 oz) whole clementines, washed

Place the sugar in a medium saucepan, add in 750 ml (25½ fl oz) water and bring to a boil. Add the star anise and the clementines, then make a cartouche. Place this over the top, along with a plate, to weight the fruit down and make sure it's fully submerged. Simmer for about 2.5–3 hours, until the fruit is completely soft and giving. Allow the fruit to cool before fishing it out, breaking it open to remove the seeds and then blending to a smooth puree, slowly adding in enough of the cooking liquor to result in a thick-ish puree that has a silky shine to it. This puree will last for weeks and weeks in the fridge, but also freezes well. Reserve the syrup for a soda (page 245).

Use 100 g (3½ oz) puree per lassi.

Rhubarb and black pepper

MAKES 650 G (1 LB 7 OZ) PUREE

Some ingredients became lassi flavours with intent, but most came about because of availability of produce, and this was definitely the latter. My favourite farmer is a man called Phil, who has an organic farm in the Southern Highlands and grows the best rhubarb I have ever tasted. It's also always an excellent deep shade of dark pink, which makes for a very pretty drink. I had been trying to find a way to slip rhubarb into Lankan flavours, and this seemed like a clever option.

4 rhubarb stalks, cut into 8 cm (3¼ in) pieces (approximate weight 620 g/1 lb 6 oz)

5 fresh bay leaves

500 g (1 lb 2 oz) caster (superfine) sugar

5 g (⅕ oz) black peppercorns

Place the rhubarb in a mixing bowl, lightly crush the bay leaves and add, along with the sugar and peppercorns. Toss well to mix and let this sit for an hour.

Preheat the oven to 150°C (300°F). Transfer the rhubarb mix, along with any juices, to a baking dish, ensuring the rhubarb sits in a single layer. Cover with a sheet of baking paper and then top with foil and cook until the rhubarb softens, about 20–30 minutes.

Remove from the oven, discard the foil and baking paper and allow the mix to cool. Once cooled, fish out the bay leaves and discard, then blend everything together until you have a smooth puree. This puree will last for weeks and weeks in the fridge, but also freezes well.

Use 120 g (4½ oz) puree and 10 ml (¼ fl oz) kithul per lassi.

Tamarind iced tea

MAKES APPROXIMATELY 900 ML (30½ FL OZ)

I am a confirmed tea drinker but only very recently have I discovered the delights of an iced one. I think it's because I had only really tried commercial versions, super sweet nonsense with strange added extras like peach, which is just weird. What I do at home is keep the remains of tea from a pot, put it in a bottle in the fridge and then drink it over ice, no milk and no sugar, the same way I drink normal tea. That doesn't really work as a recipe though, so here I have the one we made at LFS, which is neither too sweet nor weird and uses a strong black tea as its base. I find this a lovely, slightly sour, refreshing drink, and a perfect accompaniment to food.

15 g (½ oz) strong black tea leaves (I prefer a breakfast tea)

45 g (1½ oz) tamarind paste

30 g (1 oz) soft brown sugar

lime wedges, to garnish

Place 1 litre (32 fl oz) of water in a saucepan and bring to a boil. Once boiled, remove from the heat, add your tea leaves and allow to steep for 5 minutes.

Whisk in the tamarind and sugar until well mixed, and then strain through a fine sieve into an appropriate storing vessel.

Set aside to cool and then place in fridge. The tea is ready to serve once cold, but it can be kept in the fridge for a good week or so.

Serve in a tall glass over ice with a wedge of lime squeezed in and to garnish.

Coffee and coconut slushie

MAKES 180 ML (6 FL OZ) COFFEE SYRUP

I'm not sure if everyone else knew these two flavours worked so well together and just didn't tell me or if it's a relatively new combination in the zeitgeist. Or perhaps it's just a southeast Asian thing that has somehow slipped past me. I only discovered it when I went into a Vietnamese-owned juice shop and saw this combination as a slushie. It was a stinking hot day, and this cold, refreshing and perky drink enlivened me. So here is my version. It does involve a certain amount of faffing, as you need to make a coffee syrup, but it really is worth it and on the plus side, a sweet coffee syrup is a good starting point for a cocktail, too. An easier way to get this flavour fix is to combine equal parts cold coffee and coconut water and drink over ice, which is what I drink in the restaurant when I'm working and it's hot. This version is more fun, though.

60 ml (2 fl oz) coffee, cold

60 ml (2 fl oz) coconut cream

60 ml (2 fl oz) coconut water

120 g (4½ oz) ice

COFFEE SYRUP

500 ml (17 fl oz) black filter coffee

50 g (1¾ oz) jaggery, grated or finely chopped

To make the syrup, simmer the coffee and jaggery together for about 20 minutes over a medium heat, until thick and syrupy and reduced by two thirds. Set aside to cool.

To make the slushie, combine all the ingredients with 30 ml (1 fl oz) of the coffee syrup and blend until you have an even, icy consistency. Serve in a large tall glass with a straw.

Cocktails

As I have said, I'm a classic cocktail lady. I like mine ice cold, strong, not too sweet, and uncomplicated. Life isn't always as simple as that, however, so I give you some exceptions. Some are good to start or end a meal with, some to drink with a meal, while others are best enjoyed by a pool on a tropical island.

Acharu martini

MAKES 1

My two favourite snacks as a child were olives and pickled onions, so imagine my delight in discovering there was a grown-up version: cocktails with these two things as a built-in provision. The first I found was the dirty martini, my drink of choice, and vodka my preference despite the purists saying gin is the only answer which, don't get me wrong, I'll also happily enjoy. I like it with enough brine to make it murky and just two olives please, no more. And then, to my delight I was introduced to the Gibson, made with pickled onions, and I was even more excited. And what is an acharu if not a pickle with a bit more spice? Substitute with gin if desired.

- Jackfruit acharu (page 50)
- 45 ml (1½ fl oz) vodka
- 15 ml (½ fl oz) dry white vermouth
- 15 ml (½ fl oz) acharu liquid
- lots of ice

Place three pieces of jackfruit acharu on a cocktail stick or toothpick, then set aside.

Place a good measure of ice into a cocktail shaker and add the vodka, vermouth and acharu liquid. Stir well until the liquor is ice cold – twenty swivels of a cocktail mixing spoon should suffice.

Strain into an ice-cold martini glass and garnish with the jackfruit. Drink immediately.

Tamarind negroni

MAKES ENOUGH FOR 5 NEGRONIS

I have a crystal-clear memory of drinking my first negroni. It was 2006 or 2007 and I was at The Bentley Bar, an excellent restaurant with a little nook for snacks and cocktails and well-trained bar staff adept at cocktail making. I was sitting on a stool perched next to a low table, looking out over Surry Hills, where it was then situated. My drinking companion was a friend who always seemed slightly ahead in her knowledge of food and drink trends. She ordered us both a negroni. This first sip was shocking, bracingly bitter and so unlike anything I'd had that its memory is still firmly etched on my tongue. The second sip was a little easier, and more easily enjoyed. And then, not so long later, we ordered another and then maybe another again, and then I don't remember ... It became and still is a firm favourite. This version is only delicately veering from the original, the added sourness of the tamarind strangely making the drink seem slightly sweeter. The amounts below are for a larger pre-batch, as it's hard getting the right amount of tamarind for just one drink. But once made, you can stick it in a bottle in the freezer and then you are only ever seconds away from having the perfect aperitivo drink in your hands.

- 150 ml (5 fl oz) gin
- 150 ml (5 fl oz) Campari
- 150 ml (5 fl oz) red vermouth
- 20 g (¾ oz) tamarind puree
- large ice balls or cubes
- large peels of orange, pith removed

Combine the gin, Campari, vermouth and tamarind puree and mix well, then transfer to a bottle and store in your freezer.

Have some ice cold glasses set up, each with a ball or cube of ice in the base. Twist in a peel of orange to each and then pour over 90 ml (3 fl oz) of the mix. Give twenty swivels with a cocktail stirrer to dilute slightly, then drink immediately.

Karapincha mojito

MAKES 1

This drink (so-named because 'karapincha' means 'curry leaves') appeared on our menu when our supplier of Sri Lankan arrack sent us a Sri Lankan white rum. Who knew they made rum in Sri Lanka? It's not that easy to come by, but that doesn't really matter, as it led us to this drink and that is what counts. Use a white rum of your choice.

- ice
- 50 ml (1¾ fl oz) white rum
- 30 ml (1 fl oz) lime juice
- 15 ml (½ fl oz) kithul
- 10 picked curry leaves
- sparkling water or soda, to serve

Place a tumbler's worth of ice into a cocktail shaker and add all the ingredients except for the sparkling water.

Shake hard to mix and rumble the curry leaves to release their flavour.

Pour the contents of the cocktail shaker into a tumbler and top with sparkling water.

Drink immediately.

Pepper gimlet

MAKES 500 ML (17 FL OZ) PEPPER SYRUP

An afternoon gin and tonic is synonymous with the tropics – one needs something to ward off the malaria, after all – but I say ditch the tonic, find a mosquito net and embrace its far more hardcore cousin, the gimlet. It's sharp with lime, and all the peppers are like extra seasoning, making this a good cocktail to eat with, too. The pepperberry in the syrup also adds extra colour giving this drink a murky slightly purple hue. (The syrup can be used to make a soda as well, see page 246.)

- 60 ml (2 fl oz) gin
- 30 ml (1 fl oz) lime juice
- ice
- lime wheel, to garnish

PEPPER SYRUP

- 300 g (10½ oz) caster (superfine) sugar
- 10 g (⅓ oz) white peppercorns
- 10 g (⅓ oz) black peppercorns
- 10 g (⅓ oz) long black pepperberries

To make the pepper syrup, combine all the ingredients with 300 ml (10 fl oz) of water and blitz in a blender until well combined. Let this sit for 12–24 hours at room temperature. Strain and then store in the fridge. It will last for ages.

To make the cocktail, combine the gin and lime with 15 ml (½ fl oz) of pepper syrup in a cocktail shaker, add ice and shake well. Strain into an ice-cold martini glass and garnish with a lime wheel.

Pineapple shrub sour

MAKES 675 ML (23 FL OZ) PINEAPPLE SHRUB

There were moments at LFS when I was the bar girl. This made me very happy as it's one of my fantasy jobs – I have visions of slinging drinks in a smoky bar and listening to people reveal their darkest secrets. I did learn (from the inventor of this drink, the one-eyed pirate) two cocktail tricks I didn't know about. First the dry shake, which is used in any cocktail that contains egg whites, or in this case the equivalent, aquafaba, both to properly combine the drink and to give it a smooth, frothy texture (as opposed to a wet shake, which is done with ice). And the double strain, which means you are being super particular about getting the clearest drink – as he said, 'instead of big ugly bubbles you get a creamy foam'. A good lesson to learn indeed. (The shrub can be used to make a soda as well, see page 246.)

- 60 ml (2 fl oz) dry gin
- 30 ml (1 fl oz) lemon juice
- 30 ml (1 fl oz) aquafaba
- sparkling water or soda, to serve

PINEAPPLE SHRUB

- 1 kg (2 lb 3 oz) pineapple, very ripe
- 500 g (1 lb 2 oz) caster (superfine) sugar
- 3 star anise
- approximately 90 ml (3 fl oz) coconut vinegar

To make the pineapple shrub, peel the pineapple, cut it into medium-sized chunks and blend to make a puree. Transfer the puree to a mixing bowl, then whisk in the sugar and throw in the star anise. Let this sit, covered, somewhere cool for 12–24 hours.

Strain through a fine strainer and whisk in the vinegar. The amount of vinegar you need will vary according to the sweetness of the pineapple and your taste, so adjust as needed. Once you are happy with the sourness, keep the shrub in the fridge.

To make the cocktail, combine all the ingredients and 45 ml (1½ fl oz) of the pineapple shrub into a cocktail shaker. Do a dry shake and then a wet one and then double strain into a tumbler. Add ice and top with a little bit of sparkling water.

Kithul old fashioned

MAKES 280 ML (9½ FL OZ) KITHUL SYRUP

An old fashioned is a simple yet perfect cocktail that doesn't need to be messed with, but of course we have. Arrack is so similar in tone to whisky or bourbon, and the slight smokiness of kithul seems like it was always destined to be the perfect sweetness for this drink. I have also complicated this recipe further by making a burnt spiced kithul syrup. You too can follow the recipe and do this; however, I also give you permission to cheat and substitute kithul straight from the bottle instead of the syrup. It will be less faffing, but if you can't find a good-quality kithul, it won't be quite as delicious.

- 60 ml (2 fl oz) aged arrack, or substitute with bourbon
- 3 dashes orange bitters
- large peel of orange, pith removed

SPICED KITHUL

- 10 g (⅓ oz) cardamom seeds
- 10 g (⅓ oz) cinnamon stick, broken
- 10 g (⅓ oz) star anise
- 10 g (⅓ oz) black peppercorns
- 400 ml (13⅓ fl oz) kithul

To make the spiced kithul, place the spices in a small frying pan over a medium heat. Toast the spices for about 8 minutes, jiggling the pan as you go, until they are smoking. Add in the kithul and bring to a boil before removing from the heat and allowing to cool. Let this mix sit in a sensible container, covered, for 12–24 hours. Once it has sat it tends to thicken so warm it again a little and then strain it and store in the fridge. (This syrup would also be good on your morning yoghurt with some blueberries.)

To make the old fashioned, combine the arrack and bitters into an iced tumbler glass, along with 15 ml (½ fl oz) of spiced kithul. Twist the orange peel over the glass, then add it in and stir to combine. Add a large cube of ice and stir twenty times to chill further.

Aunty Siviam's milk wine

MAKES 1.5 L (51 FL OZ)

This is one of the more traditional recipes in the book and was given to me, handwritten in that beautiful cursive writing that I feel is disappearing from the world. It is elaborate and long with some things that don't entirely make sense and others which may have an explanation that I just don't understand. For example, the original calls for two wine glasses of honey, which is an immediate concern – as if all wine glasses were created equal. I have also been told family tales of batches of this being started and then left in the car so as you drive, which actually makes a bit of sense, perhaps the agitation and heat would help it all along. However, this version doesn't require a car and is almost true to the original, honey excepted, because the wine glass measurement stumped me, and the method slightly though not entirely altered for clarity.

Aunty Siviam was one of my grandmother's elder sisters who I was lucky enough to meet a few times. She lived in Kandy in a rambling old house with her sister Aunty Savi. Along with Aunty Sweetie (she of the Christmas cake recipe from LF), they were the sisters from 'the second bed', a lovely Lankan expression that denotes which marriage the children were from. I remember Aunty Savi exuding warmth and sweetness, much like this drink. It is very specifically a Burgher recipe, and a drink for women in a country where the women rarely drink as a whole (the contradiction to this being all the literature you read of the Burghers indicate they were all fond of a tipple – men and women alike), and where to this very day there are archaic monk-imposed laws forbidding women to even serve alcohol.

This drink, however, tricky and involved it may be, is worth it. And despite its curious moniker, it is actually a beautiful clear amber-tinged liquid tasting of spice and Christmas and nothing to do with grapes at all. Usually it's served straight and often at (Sri Lankan) room temperature; that is, warm. At LFS we served it over ice garnished with a good peel of orange to tone down its sickly notes. This recipe makes a big batch, but if you are going to all the trouble to make it, you may as well make a lot. It will last indefinitely if you can manage to not drink it all at once.

- 1.5 litres (51 fl oz) Sri Lankan arrack
- 6 whole cloves
- 6 cardamom pods, bruised
- ¼ of a piece of nutmeg, grated
- ¼ cinnamon stick
- ½ vanilla pod, split and scraped
- 2 large oranges, zest and juice
- 6 limes, zest and juice
- 450 g (1 lb) caster (superfine) sugar, plus 50 g (1¾ oz) more
- 560 ml (19 fl oz) condensed milk
- 50 ml (1¾ fl oz) brandy
- 2.5 ml (1⁄16 fl oz) almond essence

Pour the arrack into a large container then add the spices, and the citrus zest. Cover and set aside (either somewhere in your house or in the boot of your car).

The citrus juice will be needed in 5 days' time so you can either freeze it and then defrost for the next stage, or drink it and squeeze fresh juice when it's needed.

On the sixth day, strain the arrack mixture into a mixing bowl and whisk in 450 g (1 lb) of sugar until it dissolves.

Place the condensed milk and 1.15 litres (39 fl oz) of water in a high-sided saucepan over a low heat, stirring and cooking until it comes to the boil. Briefly remove from the heat until it settles and then repeat this step twice more so you end up with a thrice boiled mix. I don't understand this step, but I dare not break the rules.

Add this warm mix to the arrack along with the citrus juice. Whisk to combine and watch as it curdles.

Combine the extra 50 g (1¾ oz) of sugar and 125 ml (4 fl oz) of water together in a small saucepan, place over a medium heat and bring to the boil. Cook until it reaches a dark caramel, about 5 minutes from boiling, and then whisk this into the arrack as well.

Cover and leave to sit overnight.

Slowly strain this mixture through filter paper into a large jar or another appropriate storing vessel. Let this mix sit for at least a week; longer is fine too.

Strain again, using filter paper, and then add the brandy and almond essence.

Bottle and store. As it sits you may find more sediment settling at the bottom, depending how long you take to drink it. Either re-strain or ignore.

Serve it like an aunty with a nip straight from the bottle, or more sensibly over ice with a good strip of orange peel.

Mu-mu

MAKES ENOUGH PUREE FOR 8 DRINKS

I first made this drink for Muu when he was getting ready to open Ester. He wanted a drink with ingredients touched by the wood-fired oven, the base note for everything he would be cooking for his new restaurant. I roasted some pineapple until it was caramelised and smoky, did the same with some limes before juicing them and then combined this with the ingredients of a piña colada. It was fruity and tropical yet smoky and not overly sweet, a grown-up version of this often too-sweet tropical island cocktail. It was delicious, but wholly unsuited to what he was doing. And so it was forgotten until five years later when I opened LFS, when suddenly it made perfect sense, especially when substituting the rum with arrack. What made it even more perfect was when our arrack supplier sent us some elephant mugs, made in celebration of the elephant orphanage they supported, which were the perfect serving vessel. Making the purees is a little messy, as you really need to cook the pineapple and limes until they are almost burnt, leaving you with sugary, hard-to-clean pans. The acids can also strip any patina you may have. Sorry about that.

PUREES

- **800 g (1 lb 12 oz) peeled pineapple, cut into chunks**
- **200 g (7 oz) jaggery, finely chopped or grated**
- **100 g (3½ oz) jaggery, finely chopped or grated**
- **4 large limes, cut in half around the middle**

PER DRINK

- **60 ml (2 fl oz) arrack**
- **45 ml (1½ fl oz) coconut cream**
- **45 ml (1½ fl oz) coconut water**
- **85 g (3 oz) pineapple puree**
- **15 g (½ oz) lime puree**
- **ice**

Mix the pineapple and the first amount of jaggery in a bowl until the jaggery dissolves. Transfer this mix into a wok and cook over a high heat for about 10 minutes, mixing regularly, until blackened and soft. Allow to cool completely and then blend until smooth. This puree will last a good week in the fridge, but it also freezes well.

Place the rest of the jaggery in a small frying pan and cook over a medium heat for about 2½ minutes, until the jaggery starts to melt and bubble. Place the limes, cut side down, on top of the melted sugar and cook slowly for about 10 minutes, jiggling the pan periodically, until the limes have a very charred face. Transfer to a bowl, making sure to scrape all the caramelised bits from the pan, then set aside until cool enough to touch. Using a hand-held citrus reamer, juice the limes back into the bowl, discarding the skin. You will end up with a black, lumpy mass. Allow to cool completely. This juice will last a good week in the fridge, but it also freezes well.

To make the Mu-mu, place all ingredients in a blender and mix until you have a smooth, slushy consistency. Pour into a large glass, or an elephant mug if you have one (currently on sale on our website ...) and serve with a straw. Sadly, no more cocktail umbrellas, as they have little plastic bits which are bad for the environment ...

Despite coming from a large family of eaters, on both sides, O Tama Carey was a very picky eater as a child. This has thankfully changed. For a long time now, she has worked in the hospitality industry and has a deep appreciation of the hard work and joy that comes from restaurants. She started working in kitchens quite by accident as a teenager after landing a job in a restaurant in London's Notting Hill. Since then, she has cooked French at Bistro Moncur, Chinese at Billy Kwong and Italian – her version – at Berta where she was head chef. In 2018 she opened Lankan Filling Station, her first solo adventure in Sydney's inner-city Darlinghurst. She travels (to eat) as often as she can and writes about food. Currently she would prefer it if someone else would prepare dinner for her and her family however despite this she still loves the food.

The fact of my Sri Lankan heritage and me being a chef were two very different things for most of my career up until I opened Lanka Filling Station. So, to all the people who helped over the years to create, influence and care for the restaurant.

And especially to the producers who work so hard, because without them there is no food nor inspiration.

And just as importantly to all the customers who walked through the doors and appreciated what we did.

And, at the risk of repeating myself, I must say that this was only possible because of all the people and things previously mentioned in *Lanka Food*. This book is merely a continuation of that one.

But, also ...

Muu, my love and partner in life who also happens to be an exceptionally talented chef, restaurateur and rememberer of all the things in all the cookbooks in our house. He is handsome, clever and a very handy resource. And to Lenny too, the next in line. He's the baby we had in the middle of writing this book and the cuteness at the beginning of the drinks chapter. He has nothing to do with the recipes, however, when he's grown up and leaves home, I won't have to do a recipe scrapbook for him as I can just give him this.

Chazzy, of course, my mum and the source of my Sri Lankan-ness.

Corentin Kergall, who goes by the name of Coco as we are all too useless at pronouncing his real northern French name. Here's a little story about him. A French boy on a working holiday visa walked into the restaurant asking for a job despite having never been to Sri Lanka and knowing very little about the food. On his first day we discovered it was his birthday. I bought him a cake, added candles and we sang. I think this is one of the reasons why he stayed with me for over five years. During this time, he learnt, travelled to Sri Lanka, ran the kitchen, managed the staff with graceful care and absorbed the spices into his blood to the point where he could mysteriously channel Lankan flavours through his fingertips with complete ease. Sometimes it was hard to separate which bits of the recipes were me and which were him.

The team at Hardie Grant, with Roxy Ryan first as all projects start with her. But foremost to me, the excellent Simon Davis who I've now had the pleasure of working with a couple of times. He is a delight to collaborate with and has a gentle and understated manner that softens his firm convictions. I love his beautiful willingness to compromise, try ridiculous things, and be a bit silly. Evi O, the glorious designer who did the jigsaw of putting it all together and made this book so beautiful. She too was a most fine collaborator, she understood my vision, created it better than I could have imagined and with such loveliness in all our exchanges. Also, to Jasmin Chua, who dealt with my slightly bossy ways with a smile and Vanessa, the recipe editor, who did the painstaking job of making sure all was in order. And to all the other HG staff whose names I don't really know who have had a hand in this laborious process of making a book happen and then getting it out there.

And the perfect team that made the scary task of shooting somewhat easy and altogether enjoyable. Patsy Niven, the magnificent lady behind the beautiful images in this book with her remarkable eye, firmness when needed and playfulness when appropriate. I decided she was my new favourite person before I worked with her and still think this even though she doesn't eat chilli. Kirsten Jenkins, the stylist extraordinaire who was always impeccably dressed, incredibly professional and hilarious in equal measures. Seok-Ho Yoon, who usually works in fashion but found himself surrounded by food, mostly silent, very effective, and would eat all the things, which made me very happy. The aforementioned Corentin who pulled all the food together, was usually first in the studio and still managed to keep a sharp eye on the restaurant. And then there was Bhagyia Chavan, our former much-loved sous chef who happened to be in-between jobs and available to help. Apart from her very able hands she also provided endless amusement.

I am very lucky to have had such fine people to work with, so thank you.

OT

D

E

F

G

H

I

J

K

L

R

S

Published in 2025 by
Hardie Grant Books, an imprint of
Hardie Grant Publishing

Hardie Grant Books (Melbourne)
Wurundjeri Country
Level 11, 36 Wellington Street
Collingwood, Victoria 3066

Hardie Grant North America
2912 Telegraph Ave
Berkeley, California 94705

hardiegrant.com/books

Hardie Grant acknowledges the Traditional Owners of the Country on which we work, the Wurundjeri People of the Kulin Nation and the Gadigal People of the Eora Nation, and recognises their continuing connection to the land, waters and culture. We pay our respects to their Elders past and present.

A catalogue record for this book is available from the National Library of Australia

Lankan Filling
ISBN 978 1 76145 096 9
ISBN 978 1 76145 097 6 (ebook)

10 9 8 7 6 5 4 3 2 1

Publisher: Simon Davis
Head of Editorial: Jasmin Chua
Editor: Vanessa Lanaway
Creative Director: Kristin Thomas
Designer: Evi-O.Studio
Photographer: Patricia Niven
Stylist: Kirsten Jenkins
Photographer Assistant: Seok-Ho Yoon
Home Economists:
Corentin Kergall and Bhagyia Chavan
Head of Production: Todd Rechner
Production Controller: Jessica Harvie

Colour reproduction by
Splitting Image Colour Studio

Printed in China by
Leo Paper Products LTD.

MIX
Paper | Supporting responsible forestry
FSC® C020056

Recipe notes: Please note that oven temperatures in this book are for fan-forced ovens. If using a conventional oven, increase the temperature by 20°C (70°F).